D0425985

Plácido Domingo's Tales from the Opera

DANIEL SNOWMAN

AMADEUS PRESS

Reinhard G. Pauly, General Editor

Portland, Oregon

PHOTO CREDITS

Otello and *Il Guarany* photos © BBC, photographer Emma Louise Ogilvy.
Die Walküre and *La Bohème* rehearsal: World Wide
International Television/Martin Rosenbaum.
Die Walküre performance: courtesy Vienna State Opera/Axel Zeininger.
Un Ballo in Maschera: courtesy Los Angeles Music Center Opera/Ken Howard.

First published in North America in 1995 by

Amadeus Press (an imprint of Timber Press, Inc.)

The Haseltine Building

133 S.W. Second Avenue, Suite 450

Portland, Oregon 97204, U.S.A.

1-800-327-5680 (U.S.A. and Canada only)

© Daniel Snowman 1994

Designed by Barbara Mercer

ISBN 0–931340–98–5

Set in Perpetua by Selwood Systems, Midsomer Norton
Printed and bound in Great Britain by Butler & Tanner Ltd, Frome, Somerset
Colour separations by Dot Gradations near Chelmsford
Jacket printed by Lawrence Allen Ltd, Weston-super-Mare

The BBC 2 television series, *Plácido Domingo's Tales from the Opera* was produced
by World Wide International Television

BY THE SAME AUTHOR

America Since 1920
Eleanor Roosevelt
Kissing Cousins: An Interpretation of British
and American Culture, 1945–75
If I Had Been . . . Ten Historical Fantasies
The Amadeus Quartet: The Men and the Music
The World of Plácido Domingo
Beyond the Tunnel of History (with Jacques Darras)
Pole Positions: The Polar Regions and the Future of the Planet

Contents

Acknowledgements

THIS BOOK CLOSELY PARALLELS THE FILM SERIES, ALSO entitled *Plácido Domingo's Tales from the Opera*, produced by World Wide International Television for BBC Television. As part of the production team, I was closely involved in all aspects of the project from the outset, and I think back nostalgically to all those days and nights closeted with Martin Rosenbaum (Producer), Donald Sturrock (Director), and Diane Sullivan (Production Manager) in some of the most—and some of the least—glamorous places in the Western world. The four of us made a happy team, and this book owes much to the support and friendship of my three colleagues.

Plácido Domingo himself was, of course, fully aware from the beginning that I would be writing a book to accompany the film series, and he and Marta were, as ever, unfailingly courteous whenever I materialized at places where they were temporarily encamped. There are inevitably one or two passages or, at least, opinions expressed in the book that I suspect Plácido would rather not see in print, but I have to record that, while helping me to correct errors of fact and vigorously arguing his corner, he has scrupulously respected my editorial independence and, for this, I owe him my deep thanks and respect.

I also owe a great debt of gratitude to Plácido's secretary, Paul Garner; so does the wider operatic world, which has little idea of how important he has been to the smooth running of Plácido's career for the past twenty years.

Thanks are also due to Peter Hofstötter and to the many friends and colleagues at the Vienna State Opera, the Los Angeles Music Center Opera, the New York Metropolitan Opera and the Bonn Opera, who will recognize their help and advice in the pages that follow.

Finally, but above all, I am profoundly grateful to friends and family who continued to tolerate my frequent operatic forays with what I can only describe as bemused equanimity. To all, my thanks, and I hope you enjoy this book!

Introduction

'Plácido, what are the most challenging dates in your diary?'

WE WERE IN SEVILLE IN 1991, AND I HAD INTRODUCED Domingo to Martin Rosenbaum of World Wide International Television, and Dennis Marks and Diana Lashmore of BBC Television. We had approached Domingo with the proposal that he permit us to make a series of films with him. The idea was to watch him at work throughout the process by which a new operatic production is born. Each film would culminate with footage of the opening night of the production concerned.

The famous brow darkened and furrowed as Domingo seemed to sense opportunities and dangers.

'Everybody has seen your performances on television,' I went on, 'and many people presume you can just fly in and perform to a near-perfect standard every time, just like that.'

Domingo nodded.

'What people don't realize is just how much hard work goes into the preparation of one of your roles.'

This interested him. Domingo dislikes the way the world's press portrays him as part of an international operatic jet set, flying around the world to perform 'his' Canio, Don José, Rodolfo or Cavaradossi with little or no rehearsal and gaining all the plaudits. Here was a chance, at last, to show people something of the effort and commitment that underpin his legendary portrayals.

I first heard Domingo in a 1972 performance of Bizet's *Carmen* given in Los Angeles by the visiting New York City Opera and was overwhelmed. Here, clearly, was a young man with a voice of gold, tall, handsome, and, unlike so many singers with fine voices, capable of acting as well. He was never out of character, even when temporarily out of the musical or dramatic spotlight, yet nothing in his singing or his acting seemed forced. He seemed to ride with the score, swim with the musical tide, gain and project strength from his inner understanding of the forces of which he was part. Never before had I heard such lyrical singing allied to such dramatic intensity. Hitherto, indeed, I had tended to consider these qualities to be mutually exclusive, yet Domingo effected a marriage of the operatic arts with such consummate skill and apparent ease.

Over the ensuing years I came to hear him perform a good many times, mostly in London, but also in various cities in Europe and the United States. In 1981, I got to know Domingo when I wrote a cover story about him for the *Sunday Times* magazine, and I went on to write a book about him entitled *The World of Plácido Domingo*, published in 1985. The book contains a number of chapters describing Domingo, in each of the world's major opera houses and many of the minor ones, as he worked on a series of new operatic productions which I was able to chronicle from first rehearsals to opening night. This was the germ that grew into the proposal for a film series and led to that initial meeting in Spain.

During the discussion in Seville, and a series of subsequent meetings, Domingo revealed details of his schedule for the next few years. He told us of a *Ballo* here and a *Carmen* there. There was the television *Tosca* to be shown live all over the world from the original locations in Rome, and did we know about the Puccini concert he was planning to conduct with a gaggle of the world's finest sopranos, or about the new Plácido Domingo singing competition to be held in Paris? We learned of the *Tabarro-Pagliacci* double act, when he would be singing at both of Vienna's opera houses on the same night, and about early plans to reunite the 'Three Tenors'.

Every one of these could make (and some did go on to make) excellent television films, but we explained that what we had in mind was something even more ambitious — not so much the glamorous events as the artistically stretching ones. We began to talk about the new works Domingo was planning to learn, the new productions of roles that extended him to the limit, and of his secondary career as an operatic conductor. In later discussions, we began to think geographically: perhaps we could encompass two films in Europe and two in North America. It was also important, we agreed, to include at least one German and one Italian opera, to choose a judicious mix of familiar and unfamiliar repertoire, and also to include one ambitious new production that he would conduct.

Thus was born *Plácido Domingo's Tales from the Opera*, a project unprecedented in the annals of film or television. Imagine footage of Toscanini or Melba, Caruso or Callas in rehearsal; what wouldn't we give to watch the operatic titans of old as they prepared new roles, new productions, new interpretations? For it is here, behind the closed doors of the rehearsal room, that all the elements that go into a great public performance are first sought out and brought together, tried, tested and imprinted. Here is the submerged seven-eighths of the iceberg, the huge expenditure of time, energy, imagination and money that the public does not see, the infrastructure upon which the entire operatic edifice depends. Until now, this infrastructure has remained largely hidden from public view — but not entirely.

In a way, the origin of this project goes back rather earlier, to a day in November 1952, the day after my fourteenth birthday, when I found myself inside Covent Garden at a rehearsal of Bellini's *Norma*. I had already been to a number of operas, mostly at Sadler's Wells (predecessor of English National Opera), and to several of Gigli's concerts at the Royal Albert Hall, and was as obsessed with opera as most of my schoolboy contemporaries were with the pop music and musicians of the day. On this particular November morning, I was on half-term holiday from school, mooching around the perimeters of the great magic factory in Bow Street I had heard so much about, and somehow managed to get into conversation with Covent Garden's legendary major domo, the corpulent Sergeant Martin. He it was who, before and after performances, would terrorize the lordly patrons and matrons of the Royal Opera House, telling them where they could or could not park their cars, chauffeurs and coats. He had a gentle side, though, and when I asked if I could be allowed to set foot inside the house that he guarded so punctiliously, he

3

slipped me into the darkened stalls, on condition that I remained quiet and unobtrusive.

On stage were two rotund ladies: the younger one a tall, well-built redhead, the older one dark and squat. I was impressed and, I suppose, surprised at how hard they both worked at the staging, and overwhelmed at what ravishing voices they both possessed. The younger woman did most of the talking, in a fluent mixture of English or Italian, asking about the doorway (I picked up 'la porta') and about the tempi to adopt. They were rehearsing a duet scene and the two sang in thirds most of the morning under the clear direction of a genial old man in the orchestra pit. Some of the scene was broad, *legato*, with long lines impeccably breathed; later, the music became more resolute, more accented, and ended (after a pair of *staccato* rising scales that had to be frequently repeated) with a high note from the young redhead.

The redhead was, of course, Maria Callas, about to make her Covent Garden début with mezzo soprano Ebe Stignani under the baton of Vittorio Gui. The scene on which I had alighted so fortuitously was one of the most superb in all opera — the long duet between Norma and her friend, colleague and rival in love, Adalgisa. I left the theatre that day intoxicated by a drug that had now irredeemably entered my bloodstream: I loved opera, and the wonderful complexity of an art form that attempted to incorporate and integrate elements of so many others. However, I was especially bewitched by the glimpse I had obtained that morning of the hard work that went into the *making* of opera at its finest. I sensed that I had been vouchsafed a view of something essentially private, secret, hieratic, the missing key, in a way, to an understanding of the art that moved me so deeply.

Over the next forty-odd years, I was to sit in on many new operatic productions, from first rehearsals to first night, and some of these were described in *The World of Plácido Domingo*, mentioned earlier.

It was courageous of Domingo, and of his colleagues in the opera houses of the world, to give me access to their rehearsals, for the performance of opera is full of the most colossal artistic challenges and risks, and few practitioners — especially among those at the top of the profession — willingly reveal to the wider public the painful and often wilful artistic endeavours that precede a first night. This is particularly true, perhaps, for singers; their musical instrument, after all, is an integral part of their own bodies. A rehearsal pianist or costume designer, even a conductor or stage director, can wake up feeling below par but get through the day with nobody much noticing, but a singer reveals his or her very essence — all the physical, intellectual, and musical impulses in the artistic armoury — the moment work begins.

There are few jobs where you are expected to be quite so personally exposed in all you do as is a singer. Opera, in particular, demands the courage and ability to pour out larger-than-life emotions, carefully calibrated and controlled. Furthermore, you are expected to be able to act in a variety of foreign languages and to coordinate all your utterances and movements in careful accordance with precise timings, determined not by your own artistic judgement, but by a composer and conductor. A singer has to look, act and sound the part, and have the intelligence, stamina and artistic sensitivity (not to mention the sheer vocal skills) to integrate all these disparate elements into a single, seamless performance.

The stakes are thus incredibly high and there is an awful lot that can go wrong. One of the popular clichés about opera, indeed, is the canon of great 'disasters' that have supposedly occurred, and, one has to say, virtually every performance contains serious imperfections in one department or another. Let us for the moment ignore the sets, costumes, lighting, chorus and orchestra, the non-arrival of Lohengrin's swan, the springy mattress visibly awaiting the suicidal Tosca. Just consider the solo singers themselves. Some people with wonderful voices are poor actors. Others simply do not look the parts they are called upon to perform. Baritone 'X' has trouble pronouncing French, bass 'Y' is too short and plump to play villains easily, while soprano 'Z' has trouble memorizing new roles. This mezzo is short-sighted and feels uneasy on a darkly-lit stage, while that tenor worries excessively about an optional high note he is expected to be able to sing.

No amount of rehearsal will give you better eyesight or added physical stature. However, many such difficulties can be overcome during a positive and productive rehearsal period, so that 'on the night' everyone is able to give the best of whatever he or she has got. The baritone's French will sound more convincing, the bass be given platform shoes and an appropriately villainous costume and make-up, while the myopic mezzo will know the stage layout better than that of her own living room. The soprano with the poor memory will have the security of a sympathetic colleague in the prompt box, while the tenor with the high note problem will have conquered his phobia with a whole string of ringing successes in the protected company of his colleagues during the previous weeks.

There is often tension in the rehearsal room. There could hardly fail to be, and it can easily take a destructive form. Sometimes, time is wasted by mere repetition or perverse or incompetent ideas. Resentments build up, alliances are formed, and all this can issue in performances that, despite the presence of star names, can be merely routine or worse. A good rehearsal period, on the other hand, with everyone pulling in roughly the same direction, can draw out new ideas from the cast, new intellectual depths and artistic heights that none of the individuals concerned could have imagined when they first assembled. The psychodynamic, the chemistry, the magic — call it what you will — is subtly different each time, but the process is essentially one that works best among consenting adults in private, behind the (normally) closed doors of the rehearsal room.

If there is any one element that can help energize an operatic cast, it is the presence in their midst of someone with the vocal, dramatic and musical capacity to lift everyone on to a higher plane of endeavour and achievement. This is perhaps Domingo's special gift, that his mere presence at rehearsal can so often inject his colleagues with that essential extra dimension of artistic imagination and achievement. 'It's a good job Domingo isn't here yet!' moaned one frustrated stage director I was watching a few years ago, as he tried in vain to get a jaded company to look as though they were interested in what they were doing. When Domingo did at last arrive a day later and the scene was re-rehearsed, the transformation was electric.

How *does* the presence of one individual artist like Domingo exert its influence on his fellows? Is it the example of his own high standards? The legendary reputation he brings and the desire in others to impress a 'star'? The gently persuasive force of his own personality? Something of all of these, no doubt. It is certainly not the result of any kind of personal assertiveness on his part. This sometimes surprises new colleagues who, awestruck by his fame, in fact tend to find him the gentlest of professional partners, self-effacing almost, a natural conciliator, happiest when part of a team and deeply reluctant to risk any kind of confrontation, even when being asked to work on what he feels is a misguided approach to the work in hand.

Much of this will become evident as we follow Domingo backstage into the rehearsal room and watch as a series of ambitious operatic productions takes form before our eyes (and cameras). In Vienna, we are present as Domingo tackles part of Wagner's *Ring* for the first time, bravely taking on a huge, heroic German-language role — Siegmund in *Die Walküre* — in the heart of the old Habsburg Empire. No other essentially Italianate tenor this century has plunged into the treacherous tides of Wagnerian music-drama as assiduously or with as much success as Domingo. However, as we shall see, this particular production was to stretch Domingo's talents to their limits.

From midwinter in Mitteleuropa, we travel to the heat and haze of Hollywood. Domingo is Artistic Consultant to the Los Angeles Opera, a company he helped to found. Here, the great tenor picks up the maestro's baton, settles himself on the podium and opens the season by conducting a spectacular production of a work he has sung a hundred times and more: Puccini's *La Bohème*. Rehearsals are intensive for what will be a highly visible gala opening, yet the maestro also finds time to put down his stick, don eighteenth-century costume and join rehearsals as principal tenor for the company's other new piece, *Un Ballo in Maschera* by Verdi.

Six months later and we are at what many regard as the most important opera house in the world, the one Domingo sings at more often than any other, the New York Metropolitan Opera. To honour Domingo's twenty-fifth anniversary with the company, the Met is mounting a lavish new production of Verdi's *Otello* with a strong supporting cast including a baritone and conductor both from Russia. The title role of *Otello* is one of the most demanding in the entire operatic repertoire and one especially associated with Domingo's art at its finest. He first portrayed the Moor in 1975 and has now sung the part close to two hundred times. But as the central attraction in a spectacular New York production of arguably the greatest of all Italian operas, Domingo knows that on this occasion even his broad shoulders have an unusually heavy load to bear.

From Domingo's 'home house' and one of his most celebrated roles, to a small town on the Rhine where Domingo has sung only once before, and the first revival in modern times of an almost unknown opera from Latin America: *Il Guarany* by the 'Verdi of Brazil', Carlos Gomes. It is directed for the Bonn Opera by the German film maker Werner Herzog. Herzog has set many of his movies at the threatening outer edges of civilization—the ideal director for an operatic extravaganza about love and death among the Portuguese conquerors and Native Indians in the forestlands of sixteenth-century Brazil. When planning *Fitzcarraldo*, his film about an obsessive operaphile in High Amazonia, Herzog asked Domingo to play the part of Caruso in the opening scene but the dates did not work out. Fifteen years later, the superstar of the operatic stage and the *cinéaste* of ultimate danger finally come together in Bonn to work on a project that, for different reasons, is a labour of love for both of them.

The abiding vision at each of these locations is one of hard, concentrated work. What Domingo achieves is not done easily. The constant striving for artistic perfection, evidently fed by an equally strong desire to bring his work to the widest possible audience, requires Domingo to call upon immense resources of physical and emotional stamina and willpower that can leave lesser mortals wilting in his wake. It can be more tiring *watching* Domingo at work than *being* Domingo at work. However, this is also a man who knows how to relax for, in addition to his wide-ranging talents as an artist, Domingo also seems to be a man genuinely at one with himself, a member of that lucky band whose capacities, needs and outlets appear to feed eagerly off each other. He seems to know when to expend and when to conserve his energies, is intensely competitive yet generous to a fault with colleagues. His patience and good humour at rehearsals are a byword in the opera houses of the world, yet so is the intensity of his performances once on stage. A man of huge personal charm with a magnetic impact upon women, yet he is a deeply and genuinely committed husband and father. A bundle of contradictions? Possibly. Yet, in many ways, Domingo seems successfully to have integrated artistic and personal qualities that, in most, remain unachieved or, at best, awkwardly at odds.

José-Plácido Domingo was born in Madrid on 21 January 1941†. He was a child of the theatre, for his parents (Plácido Domingo and 'Pepita' Embil) were well-known performers of that quintessentially Spanish form of light romantic musical known as *zarzuela*. He recalls that he and his younger sister had a happy home and childhood, though their parents' departure from Spain on a protracted Latin American tour in 1946 must have been a wrench. Things went well for the Domingos and, when the tour was finally over, they decided to stay in Mexico, start their own *zarzuela* company there and send for their children. It was not until January 1949, when Plácido was just days short of his eighth birthday, that he and his sister were at last reunited with their parents.

Accounts of Domingo's adolescence in Mexico suggest that the seeds of his adult personality were sown early. The voracious interest in all kinds of music and the compulsion to perform it, the sunny sociability, the unflagging energy, all this was evident in the boy. His formal education was somewhat restricted; when music was not distracting his attention, football and girlfriends probably were. The principal influence was, in any case, not school, but parents, particularly, it appears, the powerful personality of his mother, and it was from his parents that Plácido acquired his consuming love of the musical theatre. Sometimes Domingo was asked to sing small parts in performances for his parents' company, and he was also called upon for his growing expertise at the piano — for which he was having private lessons.

Indeed, it was chiefly as a budding pianist that Domingo entered the National Conservatory of Music in his early teens. Few of the instructors had much impact upon him, he says now, though the Chilean baritone Carlo Morelli gave voice lessons that Domingo

---

† This date, which some have questioned, is confirmed by Domingo's birth certificate (in the Madrid City Hall), his official Spanish identity card and the plaque erected at his birthplace in Madrid's Calle Ibiza.

learned to value, and, as we shall see, he also thinks back appreciatively to classes in conducting by Igor Markevitch that he attended as an observer.

Domingo's parents were quite often away from home, and it was while they were on a tour of Europe that Plácido, aged sixteen, left home and moved in with a girlfriend he had met in class. They married secretly and, in due course, had a baby son whom they called José. Domingo's formal education, such as it was, came to an end when it became necessary for him to earn money for his wife and baby. His parents, although not pleased at the turn his life had taken, gave him work in their company, and he also found himself playing the piano in nightclubs, and singing baritone parts in Mexican productions of *My Fair Lady* and similar musicals. Before long, however, the marriage fell apart and ended in divorce.

At eighteen, Domingo felt confident enough of his singing to audition for the Mexican National Opera. They told him that he was really a tenor and, to his delight, offered him a number of small roles. At about this time, he began to develop what slowly grew into a serious relationship with the singer Marta Ornelas. Marta was a sophisticated girl, more interested in German *Lieder* than in musical comedy, and, at first, she was no more attracted to Domingo than he was to her. The relationship crept up on them both, however, with all the impact of the unexpected and, in August 1962, they were married.

By this time, both were established young singers on the Mexican operatic circuit. Marta's career was more advanced, though Plácido gained local fame as presenter of a regular musical show on television. Each needed experience, however, and opportunities in Mexico were limited. Then Marta and Plácido, with a friend, the baritone Franco Iglesias, obtained just what they needed — a six-month contract to perform major roles with the Hebrew National Opera in Tel Aviv.

The Domingos went to Israel for 6 months and stayed for 30, during which time Domingo gave some 280 performances of 11 operas. If he was ever likely to have sung himself into the ground, it would have been during those relentless years in the hot and clammy opera house in Tel Aviv. In fact, Plácido considers that he left Israel a far better singer than when he arrived. Not only did he become a seasoned performer, but he feels that his proper knowledge of breathing and diaphragm support dates back to the informal tutelage he received from Marta and Franco during their days in Israel.

When the Domingos left Tel Aviv in the summer of 1965, Marta was pregnant. After an emotional visit to Spain (Plácido's first for over sixteen years), the couple went to the USA, where his engagements soon included performances for the New York City Opera — notably the lead in Ginastera's *Don Rodrigo* on 22 February 1966, the night the NYCO opened its new theatre in Lincoln Center. In 1967 came Domingo's débuts in Hamburg and Vienna, and, a year later, he was also starring at New York's Metropolitan Opera. La Scala followed in 1969, Covent Garden in 1971, and, as Domingo settled down into his thirties, he was already one of the most highly regarded singers in the business in all the major opera houses of Europe and America. Marta's singing career effectively came to an end with the birth of their two sons, Plácido (Pláci) and Alvaro. A loving and supportive wife and mother, Marta was never content to be merely these things, and she always tried to keep the shrewd eyes and ears of an expert ex-performer on her husband's developing career and to remain his most observant and conscientious critic.

Throughout the 1970s and 1980s, Domingo continued to give a constant stream of operatic performances in all parts of the musical world, recorded the entire standard repertoire and much else besides, and appeared increasingly on television. By his mid-forties, he might have been forgiven for resting on his laurels: 'If my voice had disappeared at that point,' he says realistically, 'I would still have had a career that any singer might be proud of.' Instead, he continued to broaden the scope of his activities and to hasten the transition from star of the opera to global celebrity. By the time he celebrated his fiftieth birthday in 1991, he had become one of the world's very few entertainment megastars, recognized and fêted wherever he went, the outstanding example in modern times of supreme artistic achievement wedded to mass popular appeal.

What makes Domingo tick? What impels him to work so hard, to perform so frequently, to record as much as he does? What sort of price has he paid — physically, mentally, and psychologically — for his dazzling array of achievements? Questions such as these are

11

not susceptible to simple answers or, rather, the obvious answers —
that Domingo likes his work and enjoys communicating his pleasure
to others — can scarcely tell the whole story. Any serious attempt
to tackle the question of what motivates a figure like Domingo
must involve some consideration not only of his own conscious and
possibly subconscious motives, but also of the wider operatic world
within which he is so stellar a presence. For example, the relationship between an opera house and the community it tries to serve —
or the competing demands made on top performers in an age
of multimillion-dollar recording deals, supersonic travel and fax
machines. We are all products of the interaction between our
talents, inner drives and external circumstances and, in this respect
at least, Domingo is no exception. The pages that follow will inevitably weave in and out of these three dimensions.

Careful readers may notice phrases and paragraphs that parallel
similar passages in my earlier writing about Domingo. This is inevitable; after all, Plácido is the same person and so am I, while the
Vienna State or Metropolitan Opera are the same houses. However,
the main body of this book is entirely new: not only the detailed
descriptions of the four major operatic productions in Vienna, Los
Angeles, New York and Bonn as they evolve from first rehearsals to
first night, but also the contextual material, ranging from the
musical world of Southern California to the operatic legacy of the
'Verdi of Brazil'. Furthermore, Domingo himself has moved on
since my earlier book, and we see now an older, more mature
figure, mellower, more private, no less energetic and ambitious,
but noticeably less accessible to an adoring public and voracious
press. Tempered by a train of painful events — the Mexican earthquake of 1985, the death of his father, the near-fatal illness of his
younger compatriot José Carreras — Domingo grew perceptibly
more reflective as he entered his fifties. By the 1990s, it was characteristic that he would be conducting *La Bohème* more than singing
it, and that new Wagner roles and works with Spanish and Latin
American associations would be entering his repertoire in place
of some of the lighter, more lyrical French and Italian operas of
yesteryear. This is the 'new' Domingo — chronicled in the following pages.

Daniel Snowman, June 1994

1

Vienna Valkyrie

OR

'The Ring' on the Ring

'Siegmund heiss ich, und Siegmund bin ich!'

ON 19 DECEMBER 1992, PLÁCIDO DOMINGO, APPEARING in the Vienna State Opera's new production of Wagner's *Die Walküre*, sang the words 'I am Siegmund!' in public for the first time. Heads were shaken during the first interval as old-timers tried to think of any other essentially Italianate tenor before Domingo who had assayed the Wagner repertoire with such success. 'You probably have to go back to Jean de Reszke in the 1890s,' opined one pundit sagely. 'But he was a Pole,' his neighbour hissed as the lights dimmed for Act II.

Domingo came to Wagner early in his career, but has paced his approaches up the mountainside carefully. After just two performances of *Lohengrin* in Hamburg in 1968, he spent the next few years building his career on a solid diet of Italian and French repertoire, with occasional forays into popular arias and songs in other languages, including German. In spring 1976, he recorded Walther in *Die Meistersinger* (a role he feels he could probably not sustain on stage).

Then, in 1984, Domingo made the decision to return to *Lohengrin*, a work he has since performed a number of times with great success and which he committed to disc in 1986 under Sir Georg Solti. A recording of *Tannhäuser* with Sinopoli followed in 1988, while 1991–2 saw Domingo in several productions of *Parsifal*, among them his début at Bayreuth.

For years, people had pressed Domingo to consider the *Ring*. Wasn't his voice ideal for the heroic music of Siegmund in *Die Walküre*? And if he was worried that a heavy diet of Wagner might ravage his voice, well, they said, Siegmund was essentially only on stage for Act I. Domingo listened, looked at the score and kept his own counsel. Finally, he said 'Yes'. To Vienna.

The Vienna State Opera (the Wiener Staatsoper), one of the great houses on the operatic circuit, has been a loyal home-away-from-home for Domingo for many years. Indeed, earlier in 1992, the whole city had celebrated the twenty-fifth anniversary of Domingo's first appearance at the Staatsoper with a sumptuous new production of Verdi's *Don Carlos* and the tenor had been much fêted on and off the stage, in print, on radio and television, and in the streets of the Austrian capital. So it was perhaps fitting that he would reciprocate the long-standing compliments of the loyal Viennese by giving them his first performances in Wagner's *Ring*.

Written over a twenty-year period in the mid-nineteenth century, the four operas of Wagner's *Ring* constitute one of the most ambitious artistic projects ever undertaken: the realization in music and drama of the Nordic sagas of old, telling of the rise and fall of the gods and of their ultimately fruitless and destructive search for worldly wealth and power.

In *Das Rheingold*, the massive 'Vorspiel' or Prelude, Wagner has introduced us to the world of the gods (led by Wotan, the Nordic Odin) and indicated something of their human and subhuman interests and frailties. Wotan covets the treasure that lies glistening temptingly at the bottom of the Rhine and, in particular, the ring, and has to cheat and dissimulate in order to obtain it. With the gold he pays off the giants who have built a home for the gods in the heavens—Valhalla—to which he and his cohorts ascend as the opera ends.

If *Rheingold* begins deep beneath the waters of the Rhine and ends *en route* to the skies, *Die Walküre* (first performed in 1870) starts on earth, with the sound of feet pounding across the frozen forestlands as Siegmund flees his enemies. He seeks refuge in a simple hut held up by the trunk of an ash tree. The woman of the house, Sieglinde, offers him hospitality and the two are irresistibly drawn to each other, the more so when her husband, Hunding, comes home and recognizes in the intruder his atavistic adversary. You may sleep here tonight, Hunding says brusquely before going off to bed; tomorrow we fight.

Siegmund carries no weapons, but Sieglinde, who has drugged her husband's drink to make sure he sleeps soundly, tells Siegmund of a magic sword once embedded by a visiting stranger deep in the trunk of the ash tree. The stranger, it transpires, was Wotan: Siegmund and Sieglinde discover they are his twin children by a mortal woman, and Siegmund triumphantly wrests the sword from the ash tree at the climax of one of the most sustainedly ecstatic duets in all opera. By Act II we are above the earth in Valhalla. Wotan is berated by his jealous wife Fricka over the incestuous relationship that has developed between his illicit offspring. 'If you are really a god you will kill Siegmund,' she says scornfully. Wotan, woebegone, instructs his favourite daughter, Brünnhilde the 'Valkyrie' (in Norse mythology, Odin's maidens selected heroes slain in battle and were known as Valkyries), to counteract the invincibility of Siegmund's sword in the fight with Hunding. In a moving scene, Brünnhilde reluctantly tells Siegmund that he is to die, but assures him that, as a dead hero, he will thereafter be able to take his place among the gods in Valhalla. Siegmund replies, with profound nobility, that, as he is not permitted to take Sieglinde with him, he will not come. In the ensuing fight, Brünnhilde tries to protect Siegmund. Wotan appears, overrules her, and Siegmund dies.

In the final Act, we meet Brünnhilde's sister Valkyries, who ride across the skies delivering the bodies of dead heroes to Valhalla. Brünnhilde catches up with them, breathless. She cannot bring the dead Siegmund to Valhalla, but she has his beloved Sieglinde, now pregnant with his son — the future hero, who will dominate the third and fourth operas of the *Ring* cycle, Siegfried. Wotan arrives, furious at his beloved Brünnhilde for her disobedience. As the opera ends, he places her on a mountain top, ringed by fire, to be rescued, many years and one opera later, by Siegfried.

'I love to rehearse', Domingo enthuses, keen to put the lie to the common accusation that he is a founder member of the international operatic jet set circus. And he is clearly in his element here in Vienna, working hard on a new role and a new production. He flew in (from Japan) the night of that most Wagnerian event in recent Viennese history, the Hofburg Palace fire, and joined the cast at rehearsal the next day in a disused warehouse in the Messegelände, a huge, desolate exhibition site out beyond the Prater ferris wheel.

Each day, Domingo drives out through the cold winter gloom, finds his way along the unlit, pockmarked roadways of the Messegelände and parks at Warehouse Number 31. Once inside, he slips into a bare, poorly lit men's changing room and emerges a few minutes later in black sweatshirt, loose green and black tracksuit and, as a gesture towards the forestlands from which Siegmund is supposed to have emerged, a pair of dusty Wellington-style boots.

A red bicycle, its packing label still flying from the handlebars, glides into the warehouse. Director Adolf Dresen has arrived. Keen to get started, Dresen climbs on to the raked working platform in the middle of the warehouse, moves a chair here or a spear there. There is never time to do all the work Dresen has planned and, as the pressure mounts, he thinks of more and more production points he wants to give his cast.

It is a chamber production in a way, with sets designed by Herbert Kapplmüller that bring most of the action fairly close to the footlights ('They've got a 64-metre stage,' said one member of the orchestra, 'and they end up dancing on our heads!'). Dresen seems to be aiming at an intimate, almost 'minimalist' rapport between the characters. Intimate, but intense. This much is obvious from his own body language: eyebrows raised above piercing blue eyes and a prominent nose, and every limb permanently flexed as though for battle.

Dresen is under a great deal of pressure. 'There is probably no other repertory house in the world that would have dared undertake a new production of the entire *Ring* in a single season,' he exclaims with a nervous sigh. Even a 'stagione' house like the Met or Covent Garden, which allots proper rehearsal time to each production and then plays a run of some half-a-dozen carefully spaced performances, would normally aim to create a new production of at most only one or two of the *Ring* operas in a single season, building up the whole tetralogy over the course of some two or more years. For Vienna, though, where any one of twenty or more operas must also be available for performance every month, the decision to create a new *Ring* in a single season required a leap of courageous faith worthy of young Siegfried himself. Dresen lives with this knowledge and worries that the principal onus for getting the show on the road lies on his shoulders. 'It was touch and go whether we'd be ready for the first night of *Das Rheingold*,' Dresen admits, and he is far from confident that everything will be as it should be by the time *Die Walküre* is scheduled to open.

Dresen, unlike many German directors, especially those who, like him, learned their trade in Communist East Germany, claims to be averse to what he calls 'concept' opera. To him, what is important is to create a show that works dramatically on stage. 'Concepts', he says, must be subsidiary to this end, but admits that you cannot produce so monumental and challenging a work as Wagner's *Ring* with no overall view of the piece.

To Dresen, struck by the way the work begins and ends in the depths of the Rhine, the *Ring* is about seasonality, the recurrent cycles of nature. 'It's a great problem, how to portray "nature" on the stage in Wagner's works,' he says. 'The action is always going on under the water, in the clouds, on mountain tops, in forests, whatever.' Eschewing any hint of epic or filmic realism, Dresen has gone for the simple idea that each of the works (other than the 'Vorspiel', *Das Rheingold*) stands for one of the seasons of the year. *Siegfried*, for example, will be set in the spring, with much budding greenery suggested; Siegfried himself is, after all, a naive young man in the spring of his own life.

Die Walküre is to be, as Dresen puts it, the 'winter's tale'. Hunding's tent in Act I is a giant igloo, and as Siegmund rushes in, he has snow swirling around his head. He sings of 'winter storms' abating as he and Sieglinde huddle together beneath the frozen moonlight. In Acts II and III, winter is omnipresent as the cold and cruel law of the gods repeatedly takes precedence over warmer and more humane inclinations. By the end of the opera, Wotan, obliged to abandon his beloved daughter Brünnhilde, leaves her exposed on a rock, which, in Dresen's staging, will be an iceberg. All this from a man said to be averse to 'concepts'.

'The importance of this production,' says Marcel Prawy, veteran 'Dramaturg' of the Vienna State Opera and a man who claims to have witnessed some 20 000 operatic performances over sixty years, 'is that, for the first time in decades, you get naturalistic acting. These people are walking and talking like people in a play by Tennessee Williams or Ibsen or Galsworthy or Schnitzler.' Which is, of course, exactly what Wagner, a consummate man of the musical theatre, really wanted. 'For the past forty years around the world, you've had sets where you didn't know if you were inside or outside; where Wagner said you should be in the woods, you found yourself instead in a factory. . . . I think this production is an important step backwards—towards the intentions of Wagner, who knew precisely what he was doing.'

In the old days, Prawy asserts with a twinkle—part owl, part imp—there was no mystery about the Wagner operas. In Germany or Austria, if you had children and wanted to take them to their first opera, you would choose something simple and straightforward like *Tannhäuser, Lohengrin* or *Die Walküre*. The *Ring* itself, Wagner's massive four-opera cycle (total playing time something over fourteen hours) was considered standard repertoire and went on tour from town to town. Nor was there any shortage of good Wagner singers. Provocative? Possibly, but the roster of singers at the Bayreuth Festival, the Vatican of Wagnerism, when Prawy was a lad in the 1920s, is undoubtedly impressive.

The Bayreuth Festival Theatre, or Festspielhaus, was built under the supervision of Wagner himself and, from his death in 1883, was presided over in a spirit of reverence by members of his family—first, his widow, Cosima, then in the 1920s, by their son Siegfried. When Siegfried Wagner died in 1930, a burst of characteristic family feuding followed as the reins of leadership fell to his young widow, Winifred. Winifred Wagner was born and brought up in England but, with all the passion of a new convert, had married not only Siegfried Wagner, but also the artistic legacy of Richard Wagner—indeed, the entire Germanic cultural tradition which the great composer was seen as embodying. When I went to Bayreuth with the Wagner expert Geoffrey Skelton to record a series of interviews with Winifred in 1969, towards the end of her life, she told us, unflinchingly (and in a strong German accent), how she had been an early friend and admirer of the young Adolf Hitler, himself a devoted and knowledgeable Wagnerite.

When Hitler became Chancellor, he continued to be a regular and welcome visitor to Bayreuth and to the family home, Wahnfried. Winifred was evidently an energetic and gracious hostess and made sure that the Festspielhaus, and the entire hillside on which it stood, were bedecked with colourful Nazi regalia whenever Hitler was present. Productions of the Master's works were appropriately celebratory and sumptuous (though the outstanding non-German artists of the time—and some brave Germans—refused to perform there).

Hitler, like Wotan in his beloved *Ring*, led his followers through misguided glory to catastrophic destruction. By 1945, his Germany and everything it stood for was in ruins. Bayreuth was closed, Winifred discredited. When the Festival eventually reopened in 1951, control had passed to a new generation, Winifred's two sons, Wieland and Wolfgang.

Under the composer's grandsons, the new Bayreuth emerged from the ashes of the old and created a neo-Wagnerian mystique perfectly suited to the post-war world. Wieland, a talented man of the theatre, produced his grandfather's operas on a great empty stage with minimal visual distraction, and the theorists came up with all sorts of hypotheses about the Jungian relationships represented by the essentially symbolic characters. Cynics sniffed that Wieland's stagings were more the product of post-war austerity than of any philosophical musings. Whatever the reasons, the Wagner mystique set in and, for the next few decades, every important production of Wagner was expected to be an 'event' and every major producer felt called upon to make a 'statement'.

Thus, there were Marxist *Rings*, Jungian *Rings*, Brechtian *Rings*, intergalactic *Rings* and post-modernist *Rings*. Wotan was variously a bloated capitalist, a Hitler figure, a child molester or a manic depressive. To one producer, the character Mime was in reality the outpouring of Wagner's antisemitism, while to another, the key to the *Ring* lay in its incipient environmentalism. The 'ring' itself, symbol of the renewability or interminability or cyclicity of experience, was represented on stage as, among other things, a great circle, like those dating back to Celtic times, or a tunnel with no visible ending. Costumes and acting styles, too, would often suggest symbolic answers to philosophical conundrums rather than the garb of human beings of flesh and blood. Unfortunately, the singers chosen to embody Wagner's gods and supermen were often quite incapable of doing justice to the monumental characters they were required to portray.

What does Prawy think of the singers assembled for this production? He is full of praise for the cast, but here, too, his thoughts wander back. 'When I was a child, there would be three Siegmunds, three Sieglindes or three Brünnhildes on permanent contract to the Vienna Opera. These were thought to be standard repertory roles. Mind you,' he adds wistfully, 'it was much harder in those days to get good bel canto singers so that the operas of Rossini, Bellini or Donizetti, for example, were far less often performed than now and, by and large, rather poorly done. Today, by complete contrast, there are competent singers and a large and regular repertoire for these bel canto composers at every decent opera house, while good Wagner singers are almost impossible to find — especially tenors.'

And Domingo? 'Absolutely unique in operatic history,' says Prawy. There have been outstanding Wagnerian singers from Italy or Spain, he concedes (and cites the Spaniard Francisco Viñas as an example), but singers in those days often sang Wagner in Italian or in their own language. This was perfectly acceptable. Indeed, most of the great operatic composers expected and wanted their works to be performed abroad in the language of the audience. We may smile when hearing of Caruso or Gigli singing *Faust* or *Carmen* in Italian or of Melchior singing *Otello* or *Pagliacci* in German, but this was common practice until not so long ago. When Elisabeth Schwarzkopf first starred at Covent Garden in the early 1950s, she was expected to learn roles like Butterfly or Violetta in *La Traviata* in English.

Today, this is no longer acceptable, at least on the international circuit. Jet travel, television and the recording industry have, between them, helped break down cultural barriers. Top musicians are expected to be almost permanently on the move from one capital or continent to another, and to be able to function in several languages. Audiences, too, are less culturally insulated than before and have direct or recorded access to the best the operatic world has to offer. No longer will those who attend the Vienna State Opera, Covent Garden or La Scala normally accept a purely homegrown production of a major work, and no longer can any singer with serious international ambitions work only in his or her own language.

Domingo therefore, is not unique in singing in several languages — the roster of many German houses, for example, includes fine singers from the Scandinavian and English-speaking worlds. But, while many northerners and 'Anglo-Saxons' seem to take operatic multilinguism in their stride, there are far fewer singers from Latin countries who have sung successfully in English or German. A few — the Spanish soprano Montserrat Caballé and the Mexican tenor Francisco Araiza — have managed this with some success, but no essentially Italianate tenor has ever assayed the core Wagner repertoire with the success achieved by Domingo. 'Unique in the history of opera, absolutely unique,' murmurs Marcel Prawy again with an air of finality.

Vienna is a conservative city, its cultural life dominated by the legacy of its glorious past far more than in equally ancient but more cosmopolitan centres, such as Paris or London. A lot of the men still wear hats and raise them in a gentlemanly gesture of greeting when they see you. Traditional hat shops, virtually a thing of the past in London, still do a roaring trade, selling brimmed, feathered Tyrolean headwear or, at this time of the year, expensive circular fur hats *à la russe*. The trams still operate in Vienna and the coffee houses, where you can sit for hours with the newspapers, are much the same as they ever were. The magnificent Hofburg Palace, the superbly drilled horses of the Spanish Riding School and the Vienna Boys' Choir give the city an air of imperial grandeur while the giant wheel at the Prater, carefully reconstructed after it was destroyed by Allied bombing, remains the sole survivor of a series of such wheels designed by a British engineer in the late nineteenth century for parks in Vienna, Paris, London, Chicago and elsewhere.

The old Habsburg opera house, standing on the famous Ring road that encircles the old city of Vienna, lives on, too, despite even more devastating bomb damage. On 12 March 1945, the Allies scored a direct hit, which reduced much of the building to rubble, sparing only the front façade. A great many opera houses all over central Europe were destroyed during the war. Some were rebuilt according to the most modern architectural principles of the time and some were never rebuilt. But in Vienna it was decided to reconstruct the opera house so that it would look almost exactly as before. Care was taken to incorporate into the new building what-ever up-to-date technical and backstage facilities it could accom-modate, but otherwise they achieved what they set out to do because the Vienna opera house feels today very much like it did a century ago. If you go into the no smoking foyer on the right of the great staircase during the interval, you will find the Viennese parading slowly in an anticlockwise direction, much as their ancestors did in imperial days. If you cross the Ring, stand outside the Wiener Allianz building opposite, and look up at the opera house between the two winged horses, you will see, now as then, a dedication to the Emperor Franz Joseph.

Vienna may be a conservative city with a conservative opera house, but it is not a parochial one. Vienna, like Austria as a whole, may like to draw heavily from its past, but it does not rely solely on its history. Indeed, you would not expect a city that has hosted the OPEC headquarters and a major United Nations complex and which prided itself throughout the Cold War on being a bridge between East and West to turn its back on cultures other than its own. The very month, for example, that Domingo is to open in Wagner's *Die Walküre*, the Vienna State Opera is also presenting works by a Czech (Janáček), a Russian (Tchaikovsky), a Frenchman (Bizet) and various Italians (Donizetti, Puccini, Verdi and Rossini), in addition to another German (Richard Strauss) and the greatest of the local Austrian heroes, Mozart, while offerings over at the more 'popular' Volksoper are equally varied and include a pro-duction of *My Fair Lady*. At the Burgtheater, Shakespeare and Goldoni rub shoulders with Kleist and Dürrenmatt, while in Vienna, as elsewhere, brisk business continues to be done by *Phantom der Oper* by one A. L. Webber.

Vienna, like Istanbul, was for centuries one of the world's great imperial cities, but was reduced by the First World War to the geographical and psychological periphery of the realms over which its rulers once held sway. However, if the great Habsburg Empire is now a thing of the past, its legacy can be felt wherever you go in the Austrian capital and above all, perhaps, in the musical life of Vienna. The Habsburgs were benign as imperial rulers go. The greatest of them — Maria Theresa and her son, Joseph II, in the latter half of the eighteenth century — have been dubbed 'benevolent despots' by the history books, rulers who attracted to their capital the great cultural figures of the day.

Mozart was a particular favourite. When he was a child, he was invited by Maria Theresa to play in the magnificent Schönbrunn Palace just south of Vienna. It was in these corridors of power that the little boy is said to have slipped on the polished flooring and been helped to his feet by Princess Marie Antoinette. According to legend, he thanked the princess and added that when he grew up he would marry her. If he had, she would not have died in Paris on the guillotine and he would assuredly not have died a pauper.

The benevolence of the eighteenth-century despots was swept away, with so much else, by the tidal wave that flowed from the French Revolution. It was in Vienna that Beethoven wrote the 'Eroica' symphony, dedicated it to Napoleon, and then, in anger at Napoleon crowning himself Emperor, withdrew the dedication. Napoleon himself set up headquarters in Vienna, at Schönbrunn, in 1805 and again in 1809, but Vienna was also the city to which, after Napoleon's eventual defeat, the surviving crowned heads and their diplomatic minions assembled in 1815 to try and reimpose order and stability upon war-torn Europe. The Congress of Vienna had little of the idealism of Versailles a century later, but the Vienna settlement was to last a lot longer. Its mastermind was the Austrian Minister of Foreign Affairs, Prince von Metternich, whose guiding principle, one shared with equal enthusiasm but less political acumen by his galaxy of international colleagues, was the restoration and perpetuation as far as was practical of the status quo ante. Metternich's new world of old-world order survived for thirty years (a hundred, some would say), and if his politics and personality lacked the gentle sensitivity of a Maria Theresa, his diplomacy nevertheless had more in common with the sophistication of mid eighteenth-century Europe than with the brutality of the twentieth.

As Metternich escaped ignominiously from Vienna during the abortive 1848 revolutions that swept Austria, as elsewhere, he no doubt reflected that the great days of Vienna were finally at an end. Not so. For, if the late eighteenth century had witnessed a spectacular burst of creative energy in the imperial capital, the later nineteenth was to see something similar. Just as Mozart and Beethoven had been inescapably drawn to Vienna in the former period, so Brahms, Wolf and Mahler (and Freud, Schnitzler and Klimt) lived and worked here in the latter. If the splendid palaces of Vienna resounded in the 1780s and 1790s to the gracious minuets of Haydn, so the denizens of a more populous capital swayed in the parks and coffee houses a hundred years later to the waltzes of the family Strauss. This era produced its own benevolent despot, the Emperor Franz Joseph, a gentle figure who was to prove far better at building his capital than at destroying his enemies. Indeed, the only major thing Franz Joseph destroyed during his long reign (1848–1916) was the thick walls of Old Vienna—unless you also attribute to the negligence of the old man the eventual destruction of the centuries-old Habsburg Empire itself.

The walls of Vienna were torn down and replaced by the Ring road—medieval to modern in a single blow. The Ring itself was to be embellished by a series of carefully styled public buildings, while everything within the Ring was to be preserved intact. The greatest street within old Vienna, one that ran from St Stephan's Cathedral in the very heart of town down to the city walls, was the Kärtnerstrasse and, at the bottom of this street, by the Kärtner Tor (or Carinthian Gate), was one of Vienna's two Court Theatres. As part of Franz Joseph's reconstruction of Vienna, he decreed that, at this point, where the Kärtnerstrasse intersected his Ring road, a brand new Hofoper (Court Opera) should be built to replace the old Kärtnertortheater. The Emperor's writ may not have extended successfully as far as Italy or Prussia, for from these directions came successive stories of military defeat in these years. But by 1869, his new opera house was opened as planned (and much criticized; its two architects both suffered sad, early deaths shortly afterwards)—and was joined over the next twenty years or so by its great neighbours up and around the newly constructed Ring road: the Maria

Theresa monument, the Museums of Art and of Natural History, the Neue Hofburg, the Parliament Building, the new Burgtheater, the pseudo-Gothic Rathaus, the pseudo-Renaissance University, the Votivkirche, the Vienna Bourse. Few major urban areas can have been so extensively replanned and rebuilt as was the Ring road around old Vienna between the 1860s and the late 1890s—a riot of construction that (unlike that undertaken a little earlier by Baron Haussmann in Napoleon III's Paris) meant relatively little destruction of existing quarters. Whatever you may think of the individual buildings erected around Franz Joseph's Ring road, like stones in a necklace, it is always worth remembering that they were constructed so that Old Vienna within the ring might live on largely unmolested, and so, by and large, it still does.

Walk towards the opera house down the Kärtnerstrasse or the Augustinerstrasse today, and you are treading streets that were once frequented by Mozart, Beethoven and Schubert. These streets converge on the back of the opera house, on the site of the old Kärtnertortheater (and on Vienna's Sacher Hotel, home of Sachertorte, Vienna's scrumptious, very rich chocolate cake). But the opera house itself, Franz Joseph's new Hofoper, was made to face not Old Vienna within the ring, but the new city opening up beyond.

Stand in front of the Vienna Opera today, with its faintly ecclesiastical vaulted cloisters behind you to right and left, and you look out over the Ring towards a nine-storey office building containing an assemblage of banks, jewellers and airline offices, and beyond it to one of the big, busy cities of modern Europe.

It is said that empires erect their greatest monuments when they are within hailing distance of their demise. Nothing the British built in India during two centuries of occupation quite compares with the splendour of Edwin Lutyens' Viceregal Palace in New Delhi, built only twenty-odd years before the British left. Similarly, in Vienna, it is almost as though Franz Joseph, knowing the Habsburg Empire to be finally doomed, commissioned his architects to pour their talent into his capital city while there was still time, so that future generations could see and value what they had lost. This is fanciful, of course, as nobody can foresee the tides of history, and certainly this was never one of the Habsburgs' fortes. But Vienna in the late nineteenth century embodied an almost prescient drive to marry the pleasures of exuberant excellence with a more reflective melancholy—the waltzes of Johann Strauss, if you like, alongside the songs of Hugo Wolf or the blazing fanfares and also the obsession with death that vie for predominance in the works of Mahler. Mahler may seem to have inherited and incorporated something of the grandeur of Wagner, but he also foreshadows the more tortured constructions of Schoenberg and the serialist composers of the Second Viennese School. Something of the same ambivalence was evident, too, in the life Mahler led in Vienna, where, as director of the opera (from 1897 until he and they could take no more of each other), he presented performances of outstanding quality, yet was constantly worn down by the internecine politics of Viennese musical life.

The politics of musical Vienna are legendary. It is probably in part a question of local style, tradition, temperament. The Viennese take their music seriously and, as conscientious guardians of the legacy of Haydn, Mozart, Beethoven, Schubert and Brahms, feel they have some right to snipe at anything less than the best. As the real men and women responsible for live performances are inevitably flawed compared with the gods of the past, there is always good sniping to be had. Mahler was much criticized while in Vienna, though he is a god today. Karl Böhm, who guided the fortunes of the opera during the difficult mid-1940s and again when the rebuilt house opened in 1955, resigned a year later in a hail of criticism. Herbert von Karajan succeeded Böhm in 1956, stayed eight years and was controversial throughout, but nobody seriously questioned the quality of performance the house achieved under Karajan's directorship. He introduced new works, brought Vienna a widened French and Italian repertoire in the original languages, and found time not only to conduct but also, after he had appointed an assistant director, to produce a number of productions himself. In the Böhm and Karajan years, the 'Vienna style' associated with singers like Elisabeth Schwarzkopf, Irmgard Seefried, Erich Kunz, Anton Dermota and Sena Jurinac, and later with Lucia Popp, Gundula Janowitz and Christa Ludwig, reached pinnacles of glory. For all this, Karajan, too, aroused enmities among the Viennese opera-going community, which his imperious style did little to abate. Karajan fell out with his own assistant director and resigned in a huff in 1964, and it was not until the arrival of Lorin Maazel in 1982 that the Vienna opera once more had a practising musician at its helm.

Having been appointed Director, Maazel was determined to act like one. In his first season, tired old productions were withdrawn, some controversial new ones introduced, performances were clustered in 'blocks' and every production allotted proper rehearsal time — and woe betide the old hand singing his 150th or 200th performance of a part who failed to turn up to every rehearsal! None of this was calculated to bring Maazel instant affection. His private life became a topic of gossip in Vienna. So did his salary, and the quality of his administrative appointments, some of them apparently made without prior consultation with his political bosses. Maazel was accused of accepting too much work outside Vienna and of not conducting enough performances in his own house. The seamy residue of Viennese antisemitism reared up once more, too. Maazel is not — well, he's not *echt* Viennese, people would say with a knowing look, just as they had done about Mahler eighty years before.

To some extent these kinds of political issues are built into the system. The Wiener Staatsoper is historically and constitutionally a creature of government. Historically, it was owned, run and funded by the Imperial Court, and it is as a direct legacy of its days as the Court Opera that it is today owned, run and funded by the State. The Vienna State Opera is now one of four theatres (the others are the Volksoper and the Burg and Akademie Theatres) run as a group by the Austrian Bundestheaterverband, a body directly under the aegis of the Ministry of Culture and presided over by a Ministry appointee. There are advantages to this system. The people who run the four theatres can work as a team, share and exchange theatrical expertise (scenery and costume creation, for example, or transportation and storage facilities), and lobby the Ministry jointly when they have grievances. Budgeting is done collectively and, because some cost-sharing is possible under the system, the money consequently available to each theatre is considerable. Vienna is an expensive city. Labour costs are steep, and the opera pays high salaries to its chorus, orchestra and its regular roster of outstanding singers and, unlike many opera houses elsewhere, gives some of them contracts that include substantial pension provisions.

The Viennese value opera more than most. This is not to say that more people go to more opera in Vienna than in many other cities, but, in the scales by which these things are assessed, the Staatsoper is a more prominent presence to the Viennese than, say, Covent Garden is to most Londoners, the Metropolitan Opera to most New Yorkers or even La Scala to the Milanese. When he took up his post, Maazel is reputed to have said that, after the President and Chancellor of Austria, the most important person in Vienna is the Director of the Staatsoper. This sort of attitude might not exactly have gone down well with Maazel's masters in the Ministry of Culture, but it did contain a kernel of truth. When I asked a Viennese friend why there seemed relatively little controversy over the huge sums of money the Staatsoper received each year, he answered by comparing it to the monarchy in Britain — one of those grand institutions that everybody feels they have a right to criticize, even if they have little personal experience of it themselves, but that most people feel the public purse should probably continue to maintain. A clever analogy, for just as there are not that many out-and-out republicans in Britain, though there are many who enjoy criticizing the royal family, so there seem to be few Austrians, certainly few Viennese, who seriously begrudge the Staatsoper its annual millions, but many who enjoy malicious gossip about the ways in which the money is spent. In one vital respect, however, the analogy falls down. Of all aspects of the British monarchy, the one that tends to be most immune from serious public criticism is the person at its head, the Queen. At the Wiener Staatsoper, however, it is traditionally the beleaguered Director at whose door most of the criticism is laid.

Lorin Maazel lasted barely two years in the post and it is a moot point whether he jumped or was pushed. For a while, in the later 1980s, the Staatsoper was run by two men who were appointed together: Claus Helmut Drese, the former head of the Zurich opera, and the Italian conductor Claudio Abbado, already Music Director of the Vienna Philharmonic Orchestra. The Vienna Philharmonic was the first completely self-governing orchestra in the world and its 140-odd members still govern their own destinies and promote their own concerts, mostly in Vienna's ornate Grosse Musikvereinsaal, a golden jewel-box of an auditorium in Bösendorferstrasse, possessing perhaps the world's finest concert hall acoustics. VPO concerts are not widely advertised. They do not have to be as most tickets go to those city elders lucky enough to hold inherited subscriptions. If this time-honoured subscription system keeps the bank manager happy, who can blame them for not changing it? There is another VPO peculiarity, too. Most of the world's major orchestras rehearse in the day and give concerts at night. Not so the Vienna Philharmonic, whose principal concerts take place on Sunday mornings. At night, its members have other things to do. For every evening, seven nights a week throughout the music season, these are the musicians who perform in the pit of the Vienna State Opera.

Drese and Abbado made a number of ambitious plans (Wagner, which Abbado would conduct, a lot of Mozart for the Bicentenary year of 1991); then musical politics reasserted itself in the form of the precipitate announcement that Drese's contract would not be renewed after its initial expiry date in 1991. For a while the twosome was replaced with a triumvirate as Abbado stayed on and Drese was replaced not by one man but by two: Eberhard Waechter, once a distinguished operatic baritone and by then Director of Vienna's Volksoper, and the controversial Ioan Holender, for long a top singers' agent in Vienna whose transmogrification to the status of 'General Secretary' provided an intriguing variation on the old theme of poachers who become gamekeepers. Holender clearly had to get out of the agenting business, but would he really be immune from the widespread suspicion of wanting to draw on his own stable of singers? Holender and Waechter clearly had a lot of fences to mend when they came into office. Their remit, furthermore, was to run not only the State Opera but the Volksoper as well.

Then, two things happened. First, Abbado accepted what is probably the most prized orchestral plum in the musical world — the Directorship of the Berlin Philharmonic, succeeding Herbert von Karajan. This would clearly mean the curtailment and, in effect, the end of his musical directorship of the Vienna State Opera. Then, in 1992, Waechter, an apparently healthy, *gemütlich* man in his early sixties, was walking in the Vienna woods with his wife one day after lunch and died. Holender, so recently one of three, was left to run both his opera houses alone. (In 1994, it was announced that, as from 1996, the two theatres would once again go their separate artistic ways.)

Something else happened during these years too: Communism collapsed in Eastern Europe. A century ago, Vienna was still the brilliant, dynamic capital of a vast, multinational empire that extended far beyond the confines of Austria. Four decades or so later, Austria had lost its empire, been briefly and catastrophically annexed to Hitler's, and emerged blinking from the nightmare of Nazism to find itself an occupied, middle-European stateling relegated to the edges of a world preoccupied with the Cold War. Yet its capital, Vienna, a head largely robbed of its body but still more or less intact, soon acquired renewed respectability as an international host. Vienna's charm, wealth and political neutrality made it, like Geneva, an attractive location for discreet international meetings, disarmament talks and the like—a city, moreover, in which visiting diplomats, oil executives, bankers and arms dealers could entertain each other lavishly in the evening at one of the world's great opera houses. Vienna bestowed upon all who visited it the warm afterglow of its much-mythologized past.

In the autumn of 1989, history transfigured the world around Vienna as one Communist state after another threw off the shackles of forty years. The first breach in the Iron Curtain occurred on the Austro-Hungarian border, not far away, when the Hungarian authorities literally cut the barbed wire fence to permit emigré East Germans through to Austria and freedom. Thus, by 1992, when Plácido Domingo came to Vienna to play Siegmund in *Die Walküre*, the road signs around town pointing to Prague, Bratislava and Budapest had acquired new layers of meaning—Vienna was once again a city at the crossroads of Europe, no longer at the edges of the map, but at its very centre.

The *Ring* came early to the city on the Ring. Indeed, Wagner could not have mounted his monumental tetralogy in Bayreuth in the first place without the help of the Vienna Opera whose artists he needed. Yes, said the Vienna management to the Master, you may have our soprano Amalie Materna as your Brünnhilde and, indeed, our

conductor Hans Richter, but in return, we expect early performances of your work here in Vienna. Thus, the first performances of *Die Walküre* in Vienna were in 1877, with real horses
carrying the bodies of dead heroes to Valhalla. Brünnhilde arrived
on a real horse, Grane, in Act II, and would continue to do so in
the *fin de siècle* Mahler production designed by Alfred Roller, which
stayed in the repertoire until the First World War.

The last complete *Ring* cycle was mounted during the Karajan
period, starting (with *Walküre*) in 1957. In 1981, a new *Ring* was
begun, with designs by Filippo Sanjust and conducted by Zubin
Mehta, but it was aborted halfway through and the new management, under Lorin Maazel, had other plans for the opera house.

It was the joint team of Eberhard Waechter and Ioan Holender
who really set in motion the new *Ring* production. They knew that
their paymasters and public alike wanted the house to return to the
repertoire system of performances, and the four *Ring* operas, like
all the other standard masterpieces, simply *had* to be available.
'When you go to an art gallery,' said one member of the management
team, 'you don't want only Rembrandt to be available for viewing
one year and Michelangelo another. You expect to be able to see
them *all* and then to make your own choice as to which you prefer.
It's the same with our opera house. We aim to make all the standard
repertoire available in any given season, and it is scandalous if major
works, like the *Ring* operas, are not on offer.'

Thus, the *Ring* of 1992–3 was to be the first complete, new
production of these works Vienna had seen for over thirty years,
and it was planned that it would remain in the repertoire for many
years to come. The ambition was to launch the entire tetralogy
within a single season and the most eagerly awaited première of all
was that of the most popular of all the *Ring* operas, *Die Walküre*.

'The more I get to know this role of Siegmund,' Domingo said
during rehearsals in Vienna, 'the more I love it.' One reason for this
was, at first, something of a surprise: 'I love it because Siegmund
suffers so much.' When Siegmund is asked who he is, he replies that
he should be called 'Wehwalt' ('Lord of Sorrow') and Domingo

notes that this is a character who has enjoyed few moments of real happiness in his life, except perhaps as a small child out hunting with his father. Siegmund's autobiographical narration early in the opera is almost entirely devoted to the savageries he has experienced or felt the need to avenge.

'It's wonderful to suffer on stage,' continues Domingo. 'Of all my roles, there are only three characters I can think of who have never seemed to experience really secure happiness: Alvaro in *La Forza del Destino*, Loris Ipanov in *Fedora*, and Siegmund.'

Siegmund provides Domingo with many challenges: vocal, musical, dramatic and, above all perhaps, verbal. Domingo is a good, natural linguist. As most of his repertoire is in Italian or French opera and as he is also an accomplished pianist, he normally teaches himself new roles at the piano without the need for expert coaching. But with German, a language he understands moderately well but in which he is far from fluent, a new role represents a major undertaking.

It is not so much a question of getting the right accent that he finds difficult. On the contrary, he is a good mimic and his individual umlauts and glottal stops sound authentic enough. 'Mind you,' he points out, 'people say that my diction is very clear so that if I make a mistake and say "der Wonnemond" instead of "dem", for example, everyone will hear it. Maybe I should mumble my words a bit more — I'd certainly get away with more unnoticed errors!'

More seriously, it is the underlying sense of the words, the characteristically Wagnerian integration of verbal and musical meaning, that at first proves elusive: the right lightness of touch on phrases such as 'Auf lach'ich in heiliger Lust', or the dark, brooding quality when he explains why he cannot be called 'Friedmund' ('Peaceful'): 'warum ich Friedmund — nicht heisse!'

Wagner's text contains many traps for the unwary: archaic constructions or syntactical anomalies that make poetic rather than literal sense and, again and again, his favourite device — alliteration.

> Durch Wald und Wiese,
> Heide und Heim . . .

sings Siegmund, and, most famously,

Winterstürme wichen
dem Wonnemond,
in mildem Lichte
leuchtet der Lenz;
auf linden Lüften,
leicht und lieblich,
Wunder webend
er sich wiegt . . .

These soft, lilting sounds need to be brought out almost as a form of instrumental colour while, later on, the harder textures of 'feigen Füchsen', for example, must be given a harsh edge as Siegmund recalls proudly how his father could intimidate lesser beings.

So, it is to the German text — the pronunciation, the meaning, the way to squeeze maximum communication out of these northern, non-Latinate sounds and constructions — that Domingo returns again and again. 'Plácido has such a *legato*, Italianate style of singing,' one home-grown member of the *Walküre* team put it to me, 'that the more broken style of German discourse, with its irregular emphases and mid-phrase stresses, are difficult for him.'

Vocally, too, the role of Siegmund is far from easy. 'He is on for the whole of Act I without a break,' Domingo points out, 'so that, although he only appears again towards the end of Act II and then gets killed, the role is in fact a very long one: almost as long as Wotan.' Domingo explains that, in his first scenes, Siegmund has a great deal of somewhat disjointed narration, where much of the colour is provided by the orchestra rather than the vocal line. The *tessitura* (vocal centre of gravity) is quite low for much of this early section (as it is for his dramatically pivotal Act II dialogue with Brünnhilde), but it needs a properly tenorial timbre or Siegmund won't sound romantic enough. He illustrates the point at the piano, and then launches into the beginning of Siegmund's one real aria, 'Winterstürme'.

'Everyone waits for "Winterstürme",' says Domingo, 'but instead of giving Siegmund his first big high notes at the end of that aria, the way Verdi or Puccini would do, Wagner has already written one or two tremendous outbursts beforehand.' First there's 'Wälse! Wälse!' (which was stunningly exciting when Domingo first opened up in early rehearsals) and then the whole 'Dich, selige Frau' passage after Sieglinde's aria, which, says Domingo, demands robust, virtuoso *Heldentenor* vocalism. Thus, by the time 'Winterstürme' finally arrives, it is almost restrained *Lieder* singing that's required—alongside the most exquisite orchestration. As examples of the subtlety of Wagner's writing here, Domingo singles out the delicate triplets above the cello writing at the beginning, for example, or the dotted 'Valkyrie' rhythms in the tenor line ('like Beethoven's Seventh'). Also, the whole piece comes and goes, he laughs, almost before the audience has realized it.

Dramatically and musically, this structure makes perfect sense, Domingo acknowledges, though vocally it is tough on the tenor. 'It's like a lot of Wagner in that the narrative and lyrical passages aren't spaced quite the way you might expect.' He cites the third Act of *Lohengrin*, where the tenor has a lyrical love duet early on, then at the end, two important arias, but, in between, a long, almost recitative section with the King. This he finds difficult to get right—especially knowing that those two arias are still to come.

There are plenty more vocal heroics required of the tenor in *Die Walküre* after 'Winterstürme'. Indeed, the final fifteen minutes or so of Act I must rank as among the most sustainedly rhapsodic passages of music ever written (with the tenor *tessitura* tightened up a couple of notches). By now, Wagner's lustrous orchestration is let fully off the leash and, as Domingo and his Sieglinde, Waltraud Meier, rehearse these pages to piano accompaniment, they know it will take all the considerable vocalism at their command (and careful restraint by Christoph von Dohnányi in the pit) if they are to ride Wagner's surging instrumental textures successfully.

Throughout his career, Domingo has been warned of the dangers of undertaking the heavier roles in the tenor repertoire. He was just short of 35 when he sang his first *Otello* and critics at the time predicted that the role would ruin his voice for more obviously lyrical operas like *Bohème* and *Ballo*. Yet clearly it did not. 'On the contrary,' he says, 'I still find that when I undertake one of these so-called heavier roles, it seems to free the upper register of my voice so that after a run of *Otello*, for example, I feel all the more fresh on top. And I sense that it will be the same with *Walküre*. A role like Siegmund, although long and demanding, has few high notes so that, while the middle register of the voice, the *passaggio*, is being used all the time, the top is being rested in a way.'

The purely physical aspects of music-making have great appeal and many are fascinated by, for example, how high or low or loud or fast or often someone sings. Nor are these attitudes confined to singing. Many of the most celebrated instrumental performers, too, have been those with (among other more sophisticated skills) the most formidable technical accomplishment—the Paganinis, Liszts and their successors, capable of producing more sounds faster, higher or louder than is given to ordinary mortals. However, it is to singers, particularly those at the top end of the voice range, that many direct this somewhat basic approach. The most famous and highly rewarded singers have often been those capable of pushing their physical resources to perform in a range beyond the point at which most people would feel hysteria or strangulation, to produce, against the odds, beautiful, controlled sound. We can all sing a little. Yet, just as we marvel at the athlete who can jump higher or run faster than anyone else, so there is something particularly exciting in seeing and hearing a human being able to push the voice up and beyond the range available to the rest of us.

Thus, the view of the 'singer-as-athelete' is not entirely inappropriate inasmuch as a good singer is capable of physical feats, necessarily grounded on robust good health, that most could not emulate. All this is particularly applicable to the tenor. Of the other high voices, the castrato is no longer with us, while the counter-tenor and high soprano tend to be lauded more for the controlled accuracy than the muscularity of their top notes. There is something exhilarating, for singer and listener alike, about a powerful, reverberant, chest-toned high note from a good tenor—something assertive too, as though the singer were requiring and displaying confidence and courage similar to those of an athlete approaching and clearing a high bar.

The tenor, capable of singing notes other men cannot reach or at best screech, is also invested with something of the mystique of the circus performer — almost as though he were a sort of Strong Man, Trapeze Artist or Circus Freak: 'Here, ladies and gentlemen, before your very eyes and ears, is a man just like the rest of us, yet capable of the most prodigious feats of vocal prowess while managing to retain control throughout.' Control throughout? Normally, yes, but part of the audience thrill is the feeling, the fear (perhaps even the repressed hope) that he may just possibly lose control. Nobody consciously wants the high-wire artist to lose his hold, but part of the undoubted fun of the fair is the knowledge that he *could*.

Similarly, part of the thrill of hearing a singer pushing his voice up beyond the normal limits is the repressed anticipation that the voice might break. The most emotionally loaded moments in the opera house can often be when the tenor approaches the big note of the evening. Will he make it? Will he sustain it? It requires temerity for a man to propel his voice, with full steam as it were, up and up, in public. As most men try to sing high, the voice tends to become constricted, they close up the back of the throat for fear of what might come out if they continued to apply full power and leave the instrument open, or they simply opt out and sing *falsetto*. The professional tenor, however, needs among other ingredients in his make-up a large pinch of courage, the preparedness to leave everything big and wide open as he pushes himself up above the stave. The orchestra will play a sophisticated equivalent of rolling drums during the big run-up. And lo: the tenor gets up there, stays there, and, as he comes down again, perhaps even allows a little triumphant flourish and possibly a slight suggestion of strain or even a sob to enter the voice. Everybody breathes in with him as he goes up there, releasing breath again as he comes back safely to earth.

The circus analogy is obviously a crude and inadequate way of regarding operatic singing, but it may offer a clue to a further aspect of what we may call the tenor mystique. He may be an athlete; he may even, in the eyes and ears of some, be a species of 'circus freak'. But why is it to the tenor voice that (at least since the invention of romantic opera in the early nineteenth century) most of the great surging music of love and heroism is regularly given? After all, in 'real life' men with high voices are often weedy little fellows, with less obvious sex appeal than big, beefy types with lower voices and bigger muscles. Indeed, the high male speaking voice is sometimes associated with effeminacy. Surely it is to the bass, not the tenor, that operatic composers ought to have given all their most romantic music?

The tenor voice is, in its highest register, only a degree removed from hysteria, from the frantic screams of extreme emotion. We 'raise' our voices, not just in volume but also in pitch, when we are emotionally aroused; a shout or a scream is high, not low. Whereas an unusually low timbre or low note as sung by an operatic bass is usually quieter and more resonant than notes in the comfortable middle range of the voice (and often associated in opera, therefore, with introspective, magisterial or calming modes of expression), the notes at the top end of the tenor register are often sung flat out with a fast *vibrato*. This is the stuff of emotional intensity, of heroic ardour, love, honour, anger, resolution. It is also the stuff of youth — it is older, rather than younger men who tend to have lower voices. Thus, the ardent young hero, capable of prodigious feats of arms and love — of running and jumping, so to speak, faster and higher than his rivals — has normally been cast as a tenor, the 'strong man' of the operatic 'circus'.

Not every tenor looks the part, however. Just as most men are natural baritones, not capable of singing very high *or* very low, so most are neither exceptionally tall or short, handsome or ugly. If you are unusually tall, you will probably have a long neck and long vocal cords, in which case the odds are that you will have a deep voice. By contrast, the sweet little soprano voice of a Galli-Curci or a Lily Pons, so like that of a child, seems to go naturally with a slight body, while many of the great lyrical tenors, too, such as Caruso, Gigli, Bergonzi or Alfredo Kraus, have been fairly short in stature.

Plácido Domingo, therefore, represents an uncommon fusion of physique, vocal quality and musical intelligence. His voice has a dark, burnished quality to it, covered, almost baritonal at times. He has, indeed, recorded the baritone role of Figaro in *Il Barbiere di Siviglia* and parts of the bass-baritone title role in *Don Giovanni*. At full stretch, this is clearly the voice of a powerfully built man. Indeed, Domingo is some six foot two and impressively pro-portioned with a great barrel of a chest. He has a tendency to put on weight, has broad shoulders that are more rounded than they should be, and his powerful neck can merge with an incipient double chin. But when he is in good physical shape — which is almost always and means when he is within hailing distance of about $14\frac{1}{2}$ stone (95 kg) — Domingo looks most of the parts he has to sing and play. Like many powerful men, he does not flaunt his physical strength, and moments of great vocal power are carefully rationed and attuned to the demands of the musical and dramatic situation. The real hallmark of Domingo's vocalism at its best lies not in displays of power for its own sake, but in the sense of a great instrument being carefully used. You rarely feel at one of Domingo's performances that he is pouring out his final reserves; rather, that his artistry consists of a highly sensitive and intelligent husbanding of unusually well-endowed resources. 'His appeal,' Sir John Tooley of Covent Garden once summed up for me, 'lies not only in his outstanding natural gifts, but in his capacity to control and direct them and never to be at their mercy.'

A comparison with another great tenor of modern times, one of the fellow few to straddle the Italian and German repertoire, is instructive. Where Jon Vickers in his prime would almost always give the impression that this performance of *Fidelio, Otello, Pagliacci, Peter Grimes* or *Tristan* was the one into which he had squeezed his last drop of emotional energy (though, of course, it was not and he would give the same impression three nights later), Domingo's performances tend to be more measured, the greatest bursts of artistic energy kept in reserve for appropriate moments. As with Vickers, one of Domingo's performances is always exciting in a physical way; there is a yearning quality to much of his lyrical singing that tugs at the heart, and the great climaxes of triumph or despair are superbly portrayed by voice, face and body. However, the excitement is never gratuitous and is paced by the drama it is helping to unfold.

Domingo's voice has changed very little in the years since he started his international career. Where Caruso's, for example, became noticeably darker and heavier in his mid-forties, Domingo's at fifty scarcely differed from that of his late twenties. If you listen to recordings of pieces he has repeated over a fifteen- or twenty-year period — *Lohengrin*'s 'In fernem Land', for example or 'Ah sì, ben mio' from *Il Trovatore*—you will find it difficult to tell, simply from the voice, which was recorded first. Domingo's own view is that what has changed has been the depth of his interpretations, the emphasis he gives to language, the facility with which he can colour the voice, deal with difficult *tessituras* and alternate between dramatic and lyrical passages. The role of Siegmund, like that of Otello, calls upon all these skills, Domingo feels.

For all Domingo's vocal power and versatility, it is the smooth, dark, velvety sound that remains in the aural memory. The actual quality of his voice is remarkably even. If you play one of Domingo's recordings at low speed, so that the voice sounds like that of a bass, the natural vibrato remains almost uncannily regular and free of the 'wobble' that comes to afflict so many singers in mid-career. His voice has the deeper tones more commonly associated with the heavier, more dramatic tenor roles, but his sense of lyrical style puts him in a league with Pavarotti and Bergonzi. Probably no other tenor since Björling, or perhaps even Caruso, has been blessed with this exact mixture of abilities. The tone is darker, richer, more covered than the honeyed sound of Pavarotti, more nasal perhaps, but less constricted or 'jet-propelled' than his. Where Pavarotti's voice would rise above the music produced by a big orchestra with his tight, bright, pinpointed tone, rather like a flute or an oboe, Domingo's would blend and balance with it more like a horn, unless, that is, the score requires the independence of a trumpet, in which case he has the resources to oblige. If you had to pick one musical instrument that Domingo's voice most resembles, it would probably be the rich, vibrant, generously-bowed cello (it is not surprising that his hero among instrumentalists is his late, great compatriot Pablo Casals).

Does he bring anything specifically 'Spanish' to his singing? Many have found echoes in Domingo—and, indeed, in Carreras—of some of their Spanish predecessors, such as Miguel Fleta, the first Calaf in Puccini's posthumous opera, *Turandot*. Spanish voices, as Domingo agrees, do often have something velvety about them— more velvet than metal certainly. Italian voices, on the other hand, he thinks are brighter—they tend to have a sharper, more 'pinging' resonance that helps them cut through the orchestra. Velvety voices can be very beautiful, but they can also be harder to project as effectively when tired, so, Domingo says, he has to work hard if he is always to penetrate the bigger, more booming sounds of the orchestra yet not lose the essential smoothness of texture.

It is difficult to compare one voice with another, and recordings give us only an approximation of the impact singers of the past had when they gave live performances. But the question is often asked: 'How does Domingo compare with other great tenors, particularly those of the past?'. In many ways, the quality of his voice is reminiscent of the later Caruso, but without the 'protruding jaw' mannerisms and with a cleaner *portamento* (gliding from one note to another of different pitch without breaking). Possibly less heroic than Martinelli or Corelli in Italian opera or Melchior in German, without the easy top notes of a Thill, Kraus or Gedda in French, not always as passionate as Vickers, and, for some, lacking the silvery seductiveness of a Gigli or quite the supreme aristocratic stylishness of Björling or Bergonzi, Domingo's greatness lies in his capacity to combine qualities exhibited by each of these and other great singers and to synthesize into his own art a dazzling array of qualities that have rarely, if ever, been found in a single performer.

Vocal artistry of course, consists of much more than merely the sound a singer makes. Domingo's natural centre of gravity is a little lower than that of some leading tenors, yet he seems able to cope with the most demanding *tessitura*.

Then there is the question of phrasing, the capacity to sing with the breath, to let the musical and verbal meaning of the music come across without the listener being aware of the physical needs of the singer. There are times when Domingo almost seems to refrain from breathing in order to let the music flow uninterrupted. For example, if you listen to any of his three recordings of the lines sung by Manrico to his ailing mother in the last Act of *Il Trovatore* ('Riposa, o madre') he always manages them in a single breath, yet, as with Björling, this herculean phrasing sounds the most natural thing in the world.

Domingo has great admiration for Björling and, like his Swedish predecessor, he sometimes has a tendency to focus his tone on the sharper end of the higher notes, a quality that, when held carefully in control, can add brilliance and excitement to passages of emotional intensity. Domingo is also particularly good at integrating his top notes into the texture of the music that surrounds them. He will not hold on to a high note longer than the natural flow of the music permits or interrupt the musical pulse in order to help his run-up. Indeed, he will often not even pause for breath before a high note, taking it, rather, as part of the single sweep of a phrase. Like a good chamber player, Domingo knows how to integrate his own artistry into the work and the current performance as a whole.

All this is not just a technical matter of singing more *forte* or *piano*, more *legato* or *staccato*, or building up a *crescendo* from an earlier or later starting point, though all this is, of course, part of it. It is really a question of overall musical and dramatic sensitivity, of letting the architecture of a work dictate the details. Certainly, a vast work like Wagner's *Ring* can only be performed successfully if every participant, every piece in the vast complex of its musico-dramatic edifice, has some conception of the scope and scale of the entire finished product.

As the time approaches for Domingo to appear in his first *Ring* opera, he perceptibly closes in upon himself, excludes all outside activity or distraction, and gives his total concentration to the challenging task in hand. 'Once he's here, he's here!', is how the conductor, Christoph von Dohnányi, puts it.

The Vienna State Opera has assembled a cast for *Die Walküre* of not only outstanding musical and dramatic ability, but also as engaging and welcoming a group of colleagues as Domingo could wish for as he steps into Wagner's *Ring* for the first time. Headed by Dohnányi (an experienced Wagner conductor whom Domingo has known since Dohnányi's days at the helm of the Hamburg Opera), they include Hildegard Behrens, the Brünnhilde of *Ring* productions in Bayreuth, New York, Munich and elsewhere—blonde, delicately built, with a permanent smile of almost beatific optimism on her handsome features, the polar opposite of most people's image of an operatic Valkyrie; the American bass-baritone Robert Hale as Wotan, impeccably coiffed, the soul of charm and courtesy and an old friend of Domingo's from their days together in the New York City Opera; as Hunding, Vienna's own Kurt Rydl, whose voice is as dark as his personality is irrepressibly sunny; and, as Domingo's main partner, his 'Braut und Schwester' Sieglinde — Waltraud Meier.

Meier is one of the most electrifying performers on the operatic stage today. Vocally and dramatically capable of anything from Janet Baker-style Mahler songs through the seductiveness of Dalila or the love-lorn desperation of Santuzza to the cold fury of Fricka (played in Vienna by Uta Priew) or the wild passion of Kundry, this highly gifted young mezzo is here undertaking the soprano role of Sieglinde for the first time. Forget the traditional demure little Nordic hausfrau in a blonde wig; this is a redhead Sieglinde with guts — she does, after all, drug her husband's drink so that she can make love to the handsome stranger who has just arrived in their house.

'The thing to remember about Sieglinde,' says Meier, one eyebrow cocked sharply above dark, alert eyes, 'is that she's not just *any* woman — she's a daughter of Wotan, of Wälse, strong, passionate.' Yet she is also patient; when we first meet her she has, for some time, been living a life that is artificial, unhappy and constrained as the wife of a man she does not love. Does the appearance of Siegmund herald her escape?

'No. Not at first anyway. She is the kind of person who likes to size up a situation before making a decision.' When Sieglinde meets a stranger, says Meier, a man she has never seen before, she instinctively knows she has to test out his abilities and his character before coming to any conclusions about him. Someone, some day, will be able to draw the sword embedded in the ash tree, she is certain, and rescue her from her plight, but she is not sure it will be Siegmund until he actually does so.

What then, does Siegmund represent to Sieglinde?

'He's her *alter ego*. He's the reality she has been craving: the passion, love, beauty and joy she has inside her and has wanted to express for so long. At last, she can pour all these out. At the end of Act I, the borders, the limits to her life are all lifted. This isn't escape; on the contrary, it is Sieglinde finding a kind of normality, a harmony in life that has been absent before.'

How far does Meier find herself identifying with Sieglinde? 'I suppose there's something of me in all my roles or I couldn't perform them properly. I wouldn't say that Sieglinde covers me completely or the other way round. But there's no doubt there are a lot of aspects of what I am that are in Sieglinde!'

Meier, like Domingo, is a singer-actor to whom all aspects of her art are equally important and, at their best, thoroughly integrated. Ask her which is more important, words or music, and she will dismiss the question rather than answer it. 'The words are part of the music—especially with Wagner, who wrote his own texts and took great care over both the meaning and the sound of his words.'

It is not, therefore, just a question of clear enunciation, she explains. You have to think about, for example, whether to begin a syllable on the conductor's beat or just ahead of it, and this in turn will in part depend upon whether or not your word begins with a 'singing' consonant (like 'L', 'W', 'M', or 'N') or a 'rhythmic' consonant ('P', 'K', 'T'). Some phrases need to be sung very *legato*, with minimal breaks for consonants:

> . . . Mir allein weckte das Auge süss sehnenden Harm, Tränen und Trost zugleich . . .

Others (like the one that immediately follows in Sieglinde's Act I aria) need to be sharply percussive:

> . . . Auf mich blickt'er, und blitzte auf Jene . . .

Is it something that is easier for someone who is a native German speaker than it would be for Domingo or Robert Hale, for example? 'Not necessarily,' says Meier—an excellent linguist whose powerful musical and dramatic impulses are well served by a sharp, analytical mind. 'Like everything else in opera, it's partly a question of instinct and partly a question of knowledge. In this business you need both. The more knowledge you have, the more you can let out your instincts, but instinct without knowledge can be embarrassing— and knowledge without instinct can be just plain boring!'

By the time Meier arrives in Vienna for rehearsals of *Die Walküre* she is word-and-music perfect, dismissing from the outset any help from the prompter. The role of Sieglinde is the greatest challenge of her career so far. It is a big role (Sieglinde is the only character who appears in all three Acts of the opera) and there are vocal difficulties to overcome as the role shifts from a more or less comfortable *tessitura* in the first Act to a somewhat higher register later on, but she is confident. She has been preparing the role of Sieglinde for three years—learning it, moreover, as a way-station towards an even greater and more demanding Wagnerian challenge, the part of Isolde, which she is booked to sing at Bayreuth nine months hence.

A great prima donna approaching the peak of her powers? Undoubtedly, but one whose idea of a good night out is to laugh and quaff with friends in one of the casual, help-yourself, trestle-tabled *Heurige* restaurants on the outer edges of Vienna. And if you happened to wander into Warehouse Number 31 in the Mes-segelände on the outskirts of Vienna in December 1992, you might be forgiven for not at first identifying that diminutive bundle of energy with loose, russet hair, black T-shirt and long blue rehearsal skirt as the authentic Wagnerian thunderbolt she is. She almost disappears in Domingo's expansive bear-hug—or rather the wolf-skin coat that he begins to sport over his shell suit as a further move towards the creature of the forests whom he must become by the opening night.

Ten days to go and the rehearsals now take place on the stage as the various elements of the production come together. In Act I, Hunding's great white tent (the 'igloo') collapses on cue more or less noiselessly to reveal the moonlit beauty of the 'Winterstürme' scene. Paralleling this, Wotan's black tent in Act II and the grey Valkyrie rock sanctuary in Act III both rise when required so that each Act begins in an enclosed space and ends exposed to the elements. There is snow in each Act, consistent with Dresen's idea that each of the four *Ring* operas should represent one of the seasons, with *Walküre* as winter. There is fire in each Act, too, notably an eruption of smouldering scarlet-lit lava up and around Brünnhilde's glazed rock at the opera's end (which leaves Behrens covered in plastic foam when it is time to emerge).

By now, many effects have been refined or pruned. In Act I, Hunding throws the dinner table over in a fit of fury. At first,

Kurt Rydl did this with such panache that knives and platters flew dangerously close to Domingo, who was visibly startled — a great effect, but one fraught with real dangers (not least because the stage is raked down towards the orchestra with no overhang). Later, Rydl gathered up the tablecloth first, handing it over to Meier so that, moments later, it was only the table, and not its contents, that went hurtling. By now, too, Sieglinde is no longer changing costume in Act I, but wearing her blue dress throughout. Other details were much debated, but remained unchanged. Siegmund still wore a Figaro-style pigtail and Sieglinde a scarlet hair ribbon. In Act II, the lovers were still to rest against the proscenium arch during Siegmund's long exchange with Brünnhilde. Shouldn't Siegmund, who is being told of his own impending death, place Sieglinde gently down to rest and then approach centre stage so as to address Brünnhilde and the audience more directly? Interestingly, when this production was revived six months later in June 1993 as part of the complete *Ring* cycle, the lovers did indeed place themselves far closer to centre stage.

Domingo, straining to succeed in one of the most difficult undertakings of his career, participates in all these directorial manoeuvrings and retains an air of outer calm. Courteous to everyone in equal measure, apparently happy to take musical, dramatic and linguistic direction, and to make constructive suggestions in scenes where Siegmund is involved, he nonetheless draws an impenetrable circle around his own inner space as the opening approaches, spending every spare moment withdrawn from the fray, working with his score.

At the general rehearsal, an audience is to be let into the house for the first time. How will they react to the dark lighting, the modern costumes (blue for Wotan and his twin offspring and a thick fur coat for his wife), and the girlish prancing of the Valkyrie girls to the music of their famous 'Ride'? Will the fight between Rydl and Domingo in Act II look persuasive as these two old friends struggle with each other in the upstage gloom? If the invited audience at the dress rehearsal had views about these matters, they did not express them; the reaction, as is the way on these occasions, was muted, but friendly.

The queue of people hoping to get tickets for the first night began two full days and nights before the opening. Hour by hour, an orderly line of folding seats, sleeping bags, Thermos flasks, and other accoutrements to help them stand the wait materialized along the outer wall of the Staatsoper. 'This is the most eagerly awaited opening night here for years,' said one denizen of the pavement. The proof? Ticket touts were said to be planning the most exorbitant mark-up Vienna had ever known. Thus are operatic expectations assessed.

As middle Europe plunged towards the cold and darkness of the winter solstice, the wealthy bourgoisie of Vienna paraded up and down the Kärtnerstrasse in their furs and loden coats, their green hats adorned with shaving brush-style feather clusters. '*Frohe Weih-nacht*' whispered the fashionable shops as some of the last and most expensive Christmas gifts were finally purchased. Towards the end of a cold, overcast afternoon, the owners of the most fashionable hats and furs were making their way south down the Kärtnerstrasse towards the Staatsoper.

Inside the opera house, most members of the cast arrive early. Domingo is more or less ready to go on by 4.30 pm, a full hour before curtain up. He hums to himself, asks his make-up man for a little more shadow here and there, greets friends he sees in the mirror. In the corridors outside the soloists' dressing rooms, little clusters of white-coated assistants congregate, while, from within each room, there periodically emanates a reverberant two-octave scale or *arpeggio* as the singers let their voices off the leash every now and then. The men's and women's dressing rooms at the Staatsoper form the two long sides of a rectangle, linked at one end by a room containing a Bösendorfer grand piano which is available to the singers. Domingo, restless and ready to go, wanders over, touches the keys and sings a few scales up to top C and back. His voice is in excellent shape and has, of course, already been warmed up earlier in the day. He strolls back up the corridor, past his own room, and looks to see if Kurt Rydl is around.

Just along from the women's corridor is the stage entrance. Here, dark and silent, by now cleared of the minions who were hurrying and scurrying an hour earlier, is the vast expanse of the Staatsoper stage, awaiting the great action that will shortly unfold upon it, or, rather, upon its front few metres. It is only backstage, perhaps, that one can clearly see what a small proportion of the vast Staatsoper stage space Dresen and Kapplmüller have chosen to use for their chamber-scale production.

It is now five o'clock. The auditorium is humming with expectation. At the back, just below where you might expect to find a Royal or Presidential box, several hundred standees are crammed, the lucky ones finding a velvet-clad bar on which to lean. The standees have already had a long day and night and most would be dropping with exhaustion were they not sustained by excitement at what is to come.

The opera house they look out into is handsome but not extravagantly so. In many houses—Covent Garden or La Scala, for example—the colour you notice is plum red. The Vienna State Opera does have some red, but it is the whites, yellows, golds and browns that predominate. It is a brightly lit house topped by a necklace-shaped chandelier (some call it a doughnut covered with sugar) which brings out all the paler colours used in the auditorium. The velvet curtain, until recently a lightish brown, has been replaced with red velvet, but the safety curtain that normally greets you as you enter is a gold-plated representation of the Orpheus legend. The proscenium arch is mostly gold, too, and, unlike the pre-1945 original, is unembellished. The slightly austere look of the Staatsoper auditorium may surprise a visitor expecting a rich Victorian or Biedermeier décor.

The quality of what you can see and hear of the performance varies quite substantially according to where you are—a variation that is precisely reflected in the carefully graduated seat price structure, with tickets being available in perhaps twenty different denominations for each performance. From the sides far above the stage or at the back of the side boxes, the sharp horseshoe curvature means you can sometimes see very little of what is happening on stage. Also, although the Staatsoper generally has good acoustics, there are areas where even a chorus singing strongly can scarcely project its sound across the wide orchestra pit (one of the few with no overhang above), and others where the luscious VPO string sound is almost obliterated by the brass section. Despite these blemishes, the Viennese were surely right to reconstruct the house largely as it was originally built. The front staircase and side and front foyers are grand yet welcoming, and for anyone sitting in a reasonably central position in the house — including the privileged herd of parterre standees — sight and sound are splendid.

It is 5.30 p.m. and the lights begin to go down: the 'doughnut' at the top, then the concealed lighting in the layers of boxes that encircle the auditorium. The packed audience, variously comprised of the rich, the powerful, the tenacious and the fortunate — settle into their seats at the Staatsoper or against the bar at which they stand. Maestro Dohnányi comes out, acknowledges the applause and launches the Vienna Philharmonic into Wagner's epic. The curtain rises, reveals the white tent with its flickering fireplace, and all eyes search for Siegmund's first entrance.

What followed was an evening none present will easily forget. It was not an unqualified success; there are so many elements involved in a new operatic production and few audiences find everything precisely to their taste. On this particular evening, some evidently considered the powerful musical leadership in the pit a little lacking in the kind of *rubato* (when the tempo is varied for expressive effect) that a more romantically inclined conductor might have squeezed from Wagner's surging score. Many in the first-night audience also found fault with the production, and expressed their opinion in the cruellest fashion when Dresen and Kapplmüller took a bow. 'But that's Vienna,' shrugged a friend, assuring me that the booing was coming in equal measure from those who found the production too conventional and those who thought it too provocative.

Vocally, the evening was a huge success. Rydl as Hunding and Priew as Fricka were effortlessly commanding, while Robert Hale, looking very much like a god, sang like one, tirelessly, and carried his beloved Brünnhilde, Hildegard Behrens, safely across to her pyre at the end of a long evening. Waltraud Meier's first Sieglinde was a stunning display of the most intensely expressive singing and acting from start to finish. When she named her new lover — 'Sieg-mund!' — a palpable *frisson* of excitement swept through an audience clearly riveted by her performance.

What of the new Siegmund himself? For Domingo, too, the evening was a great personal triumph. From his first entrance, through all the difficult, low-lying narration of Act I, the great mid-Act intensities, the subtle development of his relationship with Sieglinde and on to the ecstatic first Act curtain, his artistic energy never faltered. 'I'm just sorry it's so long before Siegmund reappears!', he laughed as he came off stage, eyes sparkling, evidently keen to get straight on with his Act II entrance. Clearly, Domingo had managed by the night to absorb all the concentrated vocal, verbal, musical and dramatic lessons of the past weeks and to break out of the shell — and fly.

He spent Act III alone in his dressing room, score in hand, following the music relayed over the tannoy. Then, when it was time to go on stage to acknowledge the applause at the end of the evening, he and Meier in particular were greeted like conquering heroes. As Domingo put it, when whooping like a Valkyrie backstage afterwards: 'The baby is born!'.

An hour later, in the main foyer of the Staatsoper, flanked by busts of Mahler and Strauss, a party is in full swing, and the doubts and tensions of the past few weeks evaporate in a late-night haze of champagne-enhanced *Gemütlichkeit*. Slowly, the future takes over from the past. Christmas and New Year greetings are exchanged, and when people ask Domingo what 1993 has in store, he talks enthusiastically about the new international singing competition bearing his name that is to be inaugurated in Paris in the spring. In June, the whole *Walküre* cast will come together in Vienna one final time for a single performance as part of the complete *Ring* cycle. 'See you in six months!' they say to each other as the party drifts off into the night.

'You should come and see me in *nine* months' time!' adds Waltraud Meier in skittish mood, and reflects that, as Sieglinde has just come off stage pregnant with baby Siegfried, everyone should come out and join her in Bayreuth in August when the infant is due. 'I'll be there!' laughs Plácido. He'll be singing Parsifal in between Meier's performances as Isolde. But he may have to miss the baby shower because, between performances, he is also scheduled to fit in a trip to Los Angeles.

2

Bohemians in Tinseltown

'*LA BOHÈME*, PUCCINI'S OPERATIC ROMANCE OF THE land of poverty and good fellowship, was the vehicle in which the great singers of the . . . company gave voice to their talents last night, and it was a performance to remember.'

So said the Los Angeles *Daily Times* on 15 October 1897, the day after the first presentation anywhere in North America of Giacomo Puccini's then recently completed masterpiece. The 'company' was an Italian troupe touring Mexico that had been invited north for a few dates in Los Angeles. They offered established operatic favourites, notably Verdi's *Un Ballo in Maschera*, plus this novelty by the rising star of Italy's younger generation of composers. Nearly a century later, in September 1993, *Bohème* and *Ballo* were again on show in Los Angeles, this time as products of the city's own permanent opera company, the Los Angeles Music Center Opera, housed in the plush luxury of the Dorothy Chandler Pavilion. The two operas, played on alternate nights, were to launch L A M C O's 1993–4 season, and performances of both would star the company's Artistic Consultant, Plácido Domingo, as conductor of a new production of *Bohème*, and also as principal tenor in *Ballo*.

'La Bohème has everything,' Domingo enthuses, 'romance, humour, drama, great music. The melodies — they just flow. It's the perfect work for someone who is going to opera for the first time.' He has sung the tenor part of Rodolfo in well over a hundred performances and this was the work with which he made his conducting debut at the Metropolitan Opera, New York. Dramatically,

La Bohème is an evocation of the life and loves of a colony of impoverished young artists and writers in the Paris of the 1830s, based on the incidents and personalities described by the French author Henry Murger in his *Scènes de la Vie de Bohème*. Puccini knew this work and was aware that another musician, Ruggiero Leoncavallo (composer of *I Pagliacci*) was interested in adapting the subject for an opera. Puccini often seemed to be spurred into creative action by the knowledge that he was taking a topic that already appealed to someone else. For example, his previous opera and first great success, *Manon Lescaut*, was based on a story already set by the French composer Jules Massenet.

Puccini and his librettists adapted Murger, upstaged Leoncavallo and produced an opera that, for nearly a century now, has consistently proved to be one of the most popular music-dramas ever written. Rodolfo, the young writer, and his fellow artists are the bohemians we all were, or are, or wish to be at some stage of our lives — penniless and starving, perhaps, but full of good cheer and sustained by an unquenchable optimism. Mimì, their pretty little neighbour, is frail, innocent, uncomplicated and in love. Marcello, the painter, and his girlfriend, Musetta, are boisterous, flirtatious young extroverts with hearts of gold. All share a *joie de vivre* expressed and compressed by Puccini in a masterpiece that never fails to move.

In the first Act, it is Christmas Eve. Rodolfo and his companions live in a shabby garret in the Latin Quarter. They are cold and hungry, but one of them has brought home some money (which they manage to avoid giving to their landlord, Benoit), and they decide to go and celebrate in a local café, the 'Momus'. Rodolfo will join them in a few minutes, when he has finished the article he is writing. He has hardly started when there is a timid knock at the door. It is his neighbour Mimì . . .

'It's great to have a cast who all *look* their parts,' says Herbert Ross, a distinguished and experienced movie director (*The Turning Point*, *The Goodbye Girl*) who also has many Broadway shows to his credit. Tall, elegant and looking far younger than his sixty-seven years, Ross was originally trained as a dancer and choreographer. Now he has been enticed from Hollywood to direct his first opera. 'I've always adored *Bohème*,' he says, 'but it seems to me that to work properly it's got to have not only sets and costumes you can believe in, but also young singers—athletic, lithe and agile, like those we've got here—who care about acting and know how to move about the stage convincingly.'

Domingo agrees and he, too, is delighted with the cast he will be conducting, led by the American singers Kallen Esperian and Craig Sirianni—Esperian with her appealing blue eyes and long black hair the perfect Mimì, and Sirianni surely the slimmest and most agile young Rodolfo you are ever likely to encounter. As LAMCO's Artistic Consultant, Domingo is involved in all casting decisions and, when he arrives to take charge of music rehearsals, he likes what he sees and hears.

Domingo has long held Los Angeles in special affection and has warm memories of visits early in his international career. When he first sang regularly in the United States with the New York City Opera, he used to look forward to the company's annual trip to Los Angeles. It was with the NYCO on one of its LA visits that I first heard him sing—though not as early as the *Los Angeles Times* music critic, who wrote in November 1967, of the young tenor's performance in the City Opera's début production on the West Coast, Ginastera's *Don Rodrigo*, that Plácido Domingo 'invests the arduous title role with ringing dramatic-tenor sound, a broad dynamic scale and a most persuasive sense of character'.

It is easy to see how a talented young Spaniard brought up in Mexico and intent upon making a big career for himself in the USA would have found Southern California appealing. Here is a culture that draws together Hispanic warmth and American wealth, Old World elegance and the glamour of Hollywood; themes that converge on Los Angeles from somewhat separate directions, as it were, but which together helped provide a welcoming cocktail for the young tenor. He could scarcely have imagined in those early days how he would eventually become the pivotal artistic figure in the establishment of the city's first permanent opera company.

When Los Angeles, almost by chance, hosted that first North American performance of *La Bohème* in 1897, it was a rapidly growing town of some 50 000 inhabitants. This was the decade when the American historian Frederick Jackson Turner made his famous pronouncement that the 'Frontier' was closed, that the process of white migration westwards across to new, uncharted territories was complete—the Frontier had now been crossed all the way to the Pacific. Henceforth, Turner and others suggested, the characteristic pattern of migration would give way to the establishment of permanent settlements—along the westwards routes and on the Pacific coast itself. California, the sunny haven in the far South West, became something of an Eldorado for millions of Americans who, for the next century, would periodically dream of packing their bags, emulating the daredevilry of the pioneers of old, and set out for the much-mythologized West Coast where every kind of luxury and salvation was said to await. Here, for many, was the epitome of the American Dream, the ultimate point of arrival for all the idealists, ideologues, gold diggers and runaways who had upped sticks and taken off. For them, the 'East' represented home and hearth, norm and normality, rules and regulations, an outpost of the European mainland. The 'West' by contrast stood for all that was away and beyond, free and easy, adventurous and entrepreneurial. If you want to raise money for something in New York, they used to say, try appealing to their social conscience, their sense of guilt, their fear of what might happen if they don't give. If you want to raise money in Los Angeles, however, tell them the project will succeed beyond their wildest dreams, and that donors will be rendered even more wealthy and famous as a result of their generosity. 'Back East' (said Westerners) they're too cautious; 'Out West' (said Easterners) they're too naive. The West provided a metaphorical home for every Prodigal Son and Daughter in America; 'Back East' is where they would eventually return to.

These are stereotypes, of course, yet, in some ways, the cultural history of Southern California confirms the image. Just as the USA as a whole was on the receiving end of massive waves of immigration during the decades leading up to the First World War, so Los Angeles and its surrounds played host to literally millions of transplanted Americans in the decades that followed. Some were attracted by the glamour of the movie industry, others by the prospect of work during the Great Depression. Where New York saw dispossessed financiers out on street corners selling apples, parts of Los Angeles were experiencing a property boom and spawning the fabulous and flamboyant wealth of Hollywood. Every out-of-work writer and musician in the country (and many from abroad), every pretty girl with even a modicum of ambition and/or acting talent, every frustrated religious or political visionary—all looked longingly West, and many came.

In the wake of the Second World War, lucrative defence and aeronautics industries moved West, followed by microelectronics and computers. The physical magnificence and variety of the region were added attractions. The miles of golden beaches and swaying palm trees along the coast, and snowcapped mountains, lakes or desert inland are a rare combination—'You name it, we got it!' a friend put it to me when I first visited in the early 1960s.

By the mid-1960s, California had overtaken New York as the most populous state and, in due course, Los Angeles would overtake Chicago as the second most populous city in the nation. It is easy to caricature Los Angeles and many have done so to devastating effect, saying it is a score of suburbs in search of a city, the Dream Factory, City of Fallen Angels, Tinseltown, a city of freaks and nutcases. Once you get to Los Angeles, said Gertrude Stein famously, there's no *there* there. 'The only problem with L A,' a local booster joked to me when I first got to know the region, 'is the Four Elements.' I asked him to explain. '*Fire*: danger of; *Water*: doesn't have any of its own; *Air*: unbreathable; and *Earth*: quakes.'

It is easy, too, to speak scornfully of L A's aspiration to 'serious' (that is, European) culture. As recently as the 1970s, when I lived in Los Angeles for a period, people told me that no permanent opera company would ever take root there. 'This is a very fluid, flowing culture,' they said, 'people love to drive the freeways. They like grabbing takeaway food. They love movies. Movies *move*. Like the rides in Disneyland. Also, it's a very visual culture. It's not just films and T V. Look at the billboards, the gas station architecture. It's a culture of show, modernity, movement.'

'But there's lots of music out here,' I would reply, 'and a great deal of singing talent. Why not opera?'

'Sure, there's music, but it tends to be the latest forms of jazz or rock. Music for the movies, music with lighting effects, music built around stars — or music performed *under* the stars — music that's new, amplified, transient. That's what people enjoy out here.'

I was not entirely convinced. This was a place where, these same people liked to tell me, anything could happen and frequently did. Also, all the easy catchphrases about the cultural inadequacy of Los Angeles seemed to fly in the face of the recent history of the region. For all the razzmatazz, the Hollywood glamour and the sheer prodigality of the Western myth, there was another side to Los Angeles, often ignored by outsiders and Angelenos alike, one that also played an important part in making Southern California especially attractive to someone like the young Plácido Domingo: the presence during the pivotal years of the city's great leap forward just before and after the Second World War of a large colony of outstanding musical and artistic talent. In the 1930s, the Los Angeles Philharmonic boasted Otto Klemperer as its conductor. Those two great pivots of twentieth-century musical composition, Arnold Schoenberg and Igor Stravinsky, both lived out here, as did Erich Korngold, Hanns Eisler, George Gershwin, Ernst Krenek and Lukas Foss. Performers like violinists Jascha Heifetz and Joseph Szigeti, the cellist Gregor Piatigorsky and the pianist José Iturbi (and, for a while, Artur Rubinstein) all made their homes out here, while conductors of the calibre of Bruno Walter, Leopold Stokowski and Eugene Ormandy were frequent West Coast guests. In the middle years of the century, too, Los Angeles was home to many distinguished writers — Thomas Mann, Aldous Huxley, Nathaniel West, Franz Werfel, Bertolt Brecht and Christopher Isherwood among them — while the lure of the movie industry also brought novelists of the calibre of F. Scott Fitzgerald and William Faulkner to Los Angeles.

While Klemperer was conducting at the Philharmonic Auditorium on Fifth and Olive Streets (and complaining about its squeaky seats, noisy doorways, and dirty 'restrooms'), and Schoenberg was taking on advanced composition pupils at his home in Brentwood, Los Angeles was also the scene of one of the fastest-growing and most mythologized industries in history. Hollywood, synonymous with movies, is just one of the many scattered suburbs that make up the greater Los Angeles area, but in the hills above and around Hollywood — in Bel Air and Beverly Hills, Brentwood, Topanga Canyon and the beach at Malibu — were the fabulous homes of the stars, whose names and faces were to reverberate around a world wracked by Depression and War; men like Douglas Fairbanks, Gary Cooper, Clark Gable and Errol Flynn, and glamorous female counterparts like Hedy Lamarr, Gloria Swanson, Jean Harlow and Mary Pickford. In the early days, movies were monochrome and mute (though this did not stop opera singers like Geraldine Farrar and even Enrico Caruso from putting their toes in a river clearly on the rise). Once films could 'talk', singers such as Al Jolson, Grace Moore, Nelson Eddy and Jeanette MacDonald rapidly made big names for themselves. The Disney studio began to produce animated musicals, notably *Fantasia* (1940) in which popular orchestral classics were married to vivid cartoon images and Mickey Mouse shook hands with Maestro Stokowski. Hollywood also found a ready market for colourful movie versions of popular musicals and, in 1951, hit the international jackpot with *The Great Caruso*, featuring their latest vocal star, the Italian-American tenor Mario Lanza.

Thus, a massively popular and lucrative new entertainment industry grew apace in the 1930s and 1940s in the very city that housed some of the most creative personalities to have emerged from the ravages of Europe. How did European 'culture' and American 'entertainment' regard one another? Some of the distinguished *émigrés* viewed Hollywood with deep suspicion. It would have been unthinkable for the tall, austere and fundamentally solitary Klemperer, for example, to adjust easily to the free-flowing, hedonistic, movieland lifestyle, while Schoenberg, although in need of money, was scornful of the aesthetic compromises he thought writing for film would necessarily entail. Stravinsky is said to have joked that the best way to avoid Hollywood was to live there. On the other hand, while Hollywood may have had more than its fair share of power- and money-crazed philistines, there were those in the new industry who regarded film as a serious art form, as worthy as any other of attracting and using creative talent, and composers like Korngold or Eisler (who worked for years with Chaplin), and a great many classically trained instrumentalists were sought out by the movie companies and made the transition with little difficulty.

Both communities were severely divided and many individuals deeply wounded by the McCarthyite witch-hunts of the early 1950s, an episode that virtually ruined the careers of many artists who had (or were believed to have had) left-wing sympathies during the 1930s, such as Brecht or Eisler. However, those among the European community who survived McCarthyism gradually found that life in Southern California became more settled and integrated while the movie world was in the process of shaking off some of its parvenu vulgarity and acquiring aspirations towards authentic Old World elegance. Film stars like Edward G. Robinson collected fine paintings, while it was possible for a classically trained young immigrant musician like André Previn to find an authentic outlet for his talents in the motion picture industry. Thus, an accommodation of sorts was sealed between the ostentatious wealth of Hollywood and the great reservoir of artistic talent the region attracted.

Los Angeles was never a *land ohne musik*. The Los Angeles Philharmonic Orchestra dates back to 1919, a result of the vision (and money) of one man, William A. Clark. For years, the orchestra struggled from crisis to crisis, playing in a variety of halls around Los Angeles and Orange County in an effort to build up funds and audiences. Its most highly publicized and attended concerts were in the giant Hollywood Bowl, a glorious natural setting beneath the stars (and often attended by them). Outdoor opera was occasionally produced at the Bowl, too, with over 20 000 people coming to fully staged performances of *Carmen* in 1936 and *Die Walküre* in 1938. According to one account, 'the classic "Ride of the Valkyries" was breathtaking, as live snow-white horses, twice the usual number in most productions of the opera, with twice the usual number of Valkyries astride them, galloped down a distant hill on to the Bowl stage . . . (and) thunder and lightning and smoke boomed and crackled and billowed from the mountain-top set, accompanied by the delighted and excited shrieks of the audience.'

There was indoor opera in Los Angeles, too. The company that had given the North American première of *La Bohème* in 1897 was not a totally isolated visitor to Southern California. A decade earlier,

Chatting to colleagues during a break in *Otello* rehearsals at the Met.

Working on the role of Siegmund in *Die Walküre* in Vienna (with Theodor Gress at the piano).

Domingo, rehearsing *Die Walküre* in Vienna, getting to grips with stage director Adolf Dresen (*above*) and co-star Waltraud Meier (*below*).

The singing maestro rehearsing
La Bohème in Los Angeles.

As Gustavo in *Un Ballo in Maschera* in Los Angeles.

Domingo as Pery (*Top*)

Werner Herzog amidst the Aimorè Indians. (*Bottom*)

Il Guarany at the Bonn Opera, June 1994.

Above: Mutual adoration: Verónica Villarroel as Cecilia, Domingo as Pery.

Below: Mutual disdain: Domingo as Pery, Carlos Alvarez as Gonzales.

Werner Herzog.

Patti had sung at Mott's Hall on South Main Street, the same year that Mrs Thurber's National Grand Opera Company of New Jersey had appeared at the new Hazard's Pavilion at Fifth and Olive (the location that would later house the Philharmonic Auditorium). In 1900, the New York Metropolitan Opera began to include Los Angeles in its annual tour; Nellie Melba sang *Bohème* and the Mad Scene from *Lucia* on the same bill, but visits from the Met ended abruptly after the company was caught (and many of its instruments, sets and costumes destroyed) in the San Francisco earthquake of 1906.

The next three quarters of a century saw a whole series of attempts to form a home-based opera company in Los Angeles. In the 1930s two such enterprises briefly existed simultaneously and, for a while, opera lovers could periodically expect to hear singers of the stature of Claudia Muzio, Johanna Gadski, Rosa Raisa, Beniamino Gigli, Tito Schipa, Fyodor Chaliapin, Antonio Scotti, Riccardo Stracciari, Giuseppe de Luca or Marcel Journet appearing in a variety of inadequate venues, including the Philharmonic Auditorium and the enormous (6000-seat) Shrine Auditorium. But for the most part Angeleno operaphiles had to make do with visiting companies. From 1936, the new and thriving San Francisco Opera made an annual trip down the coast to play a season at Shrine Auditorium and then, in 1948, after an absence of forty-two years, the Metropolitan included Los Angeles in its tour once again.

For all the wealth and all the glamour Los Angeles possessed, and for all its evident appetite for classical music (and despite the fact that many of the new Metropolitan stars now had pronounceable names like Stevens, Warren, Tibbett, Tucker, Peerce, Merrill and Hines), regular homegrown opera still resolutely refused to take root in Los Angeles.

At this point, a powerful new actor appeared on the stage: Mrs Dorothy Buffum Chandler, Chairman of the Hollywood Bowl Association and Executive Vice-President of the Southern California Symphony Association and wife of the publisher of the *Los Angeles*

Times. 'Buff' Chandler, a forceful, entrepreneurial woman, inspired and energized those responsible for the fluctuating fortunes of the Bowl (which she had rescued from imminent closure in 1951) and the Los Angeles Philharmonic. Her persuasive capacities among the rich and powerful soon became legendary, as did the imaginative forms of fundraising she arranged. If symphony concerts 'Under the Stars' did not always fill the Bowl, how about a 'Festival of the Americas', graced by the presence of her friend Vice-President 'Dick' Nixon? Then there were the 'Walt Disney Nights' with Disney, grinning broadly, 'hereby proclaimed Honorary Governor of the State of California' for the duration, and the Governor himself proclaimed Honorary President of the Bowl! When the gates to Disneyland first opened in 1955, one of the first letters of congratulation was from Mrs Chandler. Her shrewd courting of Walt Disney was to pay handsome dividends many years later.

Mrs Chandler wanted her Bowl to be filled to overflowing, partly to fulfil the financial obligations of the Board she served, but also because she and her colleagues had an even more ambitious aim in view: the eventual establishment, as the apex of the new Civic Center then being developed up the slope of Los Angeles' Bunker Hill, of a custom-built Los Angeles Music Center, an Acropolis of the performing arts. For a decade and more, Mrs Chandler and her cohorts raised money for this project — eventually over $13 million — from among the great and the good and the wealthy of Los Angeles and beyond. Finally, in December 1964, the Los Angeles Philharmonic, under their charismatic young maestro Zubin Mehta, moved into their magnificent new home. The orchestra opened with a brassy fanfare (by Richard Strauss). 'We like the acoustics!' beamed Mehta to an ecstatic audience. Two-and-a-half years later, in April 1967, two theatres, the Mark Taper Forum and the larger Ahmanson Theater, were opened across the plaza and the initial building was officially named the Dorothy Chandler Pavilion. Mrs Chandler's dream was complete; Los Angeles, like New York (whose Lincoln Center had been opened in those same years), had an up-to-date performing arts complex. New Californian money and Old World culture were firmly united and had erected a superb parthenon to proclaim their troth. The Music Center was, indeed, built on Temple Street, and bounded on its three other sides by

60

Grand, First and Hope. Symbolism scarcely comes more potent than this.

From the outset, the 3250-seat Dorothy Chandler Pavilion was designed to be the permanent home of the Los Angeles Philharmonic. However, it was also built with sufficient backstage flexibility to function as a theatre and, before long, found additional tenants. One of the first was the New York City Opera, whose regular autumn visits commenced in 1967 with the young Domingo starring in *Don Rodrigo*. Since 1968, the wider world has probably known the Dorothy Chandler best as the site of the annual Motion Picture Academy Awards — the Oscars.

By the early 1980s, audiences and critical support for the annual visit of the New York City Opera were dropping away, the company felt unloved, and the inevitable, somewhat acrimonious, break finally came in 1982. That year the Los Angeles Philharmonic tried its own hand at opera and mounted a costly production of Verdi's *Falstaff* in conjunction with London's Royal Opera, an experiment that was successful enough but could hardly be duplicated on a regular basis. However, the link with Covent Garden was to bear remarkable fruit a couple of years later when, as the high point of the Arts Festival accompanying the 1984 Los Angeles Olympic Games, the Royal Opera visited the Dorothy Chandler Pavilion and brought *Die Zauberflöte*, *Peter Grimes* (with Jon Vickers) and a new production of *Turandot* (with Gwyneth Jones and Plácido Domingo).

The Covent Garden visit was an overwhelming success, both artistically and financially, and it proved beyond doubt to those prepared to heed the message that there *was* an audience in Los Angeles thirsting for regular, high-quality opera, and prepared to pay for it. Domingo, already on the Board of the L A Music Center Association and deeply conscious of the huge Hispanic population in Southern California to whom he knew he was in some ways a role model, had no doubts. 'We *have* to do opera here,' he told everyone enthusiastically. In October 1984, Peter Hemmings, an Englishman who had run both Scottish and Australian Opera and the London Symphony Orchestra, was appointed by the Board to be the General Manager of a new company, and Domingo readily agreed to become actively involved in all decisions about repertoire and casting, with the title of Artistic Consultant. Two years later, with Domingo himself starring in a new production of *Otello*, the Los Angeles Music Center Opera opened its first season and went on to establish itself as the only permanent opera company ever to take root in the history of the city.

'O Mimì, tu più non torni . . .' It is late August 1993 and everybody at the Los Angeles Opera is counting the days before the curtain goes up on *La Bohème*, the prestigious and costly new production that will inaugurate the company's eighth successive season.

Outside, downtown Los Angeles is at its worst—unbearably hot, sticky, and smoggy. Inside the cool, air-conditioned Dorothy Chandler Pavilion auditorium, Plácido Domingo is rehearsing the orchestra and mouthing the words of the beautiful, elegaic male-voice duet that begins Act IV. The curtain is down and the front of the house empty and dark, except for the lights illuminating the orchestra's music stands and the score on the desk before the conductor. With his head projected earnestly forwards, dark eyes alert, huge shoulders heavily hunched, arms and baton aloft, Domingo wills the members of the orchestra along with him in this richly lyrical music. He worries that he has still not had enough time to familiarize them with the details of the score and the way he wants it performed. It is already 9.30 at night, and today's *Bohème* run-through began just after lunch and has barely one hour to go. This is a constant refrain with Domingo: 'Time, time, you don't ever have enough time *really* to work. When you are in a rehearsal with the orchestra, you would like to stop to correct things, but there is never enough time. One tries to do the best one can, but it's always at the back of your mind that you'd like to stop and do more.' At the *Sitzprobe*, the first big opportunity for a complete musical run-through of *Bohème* with soloists, chorus, and orchestra unencumbered by production considerations, which took place a week earlier, Domingo began by rehearsing Acts II and III, was able to dismiss the chorus at the break, went on to Act IV — but never made it to Act I.

By now, however, music and production are coming together. In the pit, wearing jeans and a casual blue shirt (his fourth today),

Domingo takes off his glasses, wipes his brow on a towel he keeps nearby, and discusses one of the finer points with the Concert Master to his left. The members of the Los Angeles Chamber Orchestra wait patiently. 'O K,' he says, looking up and raising his baton once more, 'back to the beginning of the Act again please.'

Act I V starts with a fast *allegro* in $\frac{3}{8}$ time, a cheeky off-the-beat three-note descending scale that is the instant hallmark of *La Bohème*. Six hours ago, these same notes heralded the beginning of the opera.

As the curtain rises on Act I V, the two principal men, the tenor and baritone, Rodolfo the poet and Marcello the painter, indulge in an apparently casual but precisely timed exchange of comments, constantly counterpointed by impressionistic bursts of orchestral colour that later graduate into a great romantic *legato*, followed by the main melody of their duet. The rhythms of this opening section are not easy to play and the passage is punctuated by periodic pauses from which the orchestra must be sure to lift off together. Then there is the sweeping introduction to the duet proper, during which the orchestra must throb with romantic longing, but not so forcefully as to diminish the impact of the singers who have to take over from it.

Each of these brief sections needs careful orchestral rehearsal, Domingo feels, before he can ask for the curtain to be raised and for his singers — Craig Sirianni and the Australian baritone Jeffrey Black, both waiting patiently on stage — to join in the proceedings. Like any good conductor, Domingo is thoroughly familiar with the vocal parts and quietly provides the quicksilver lines of the two soloists himself as he puts the orchestra through its paces. After a number of false starts, they finally reach the big tune once again. This time the strings surge up magnificently and Domingo can no longer restrain himself: 'O Mimì, tu più non torni, O giorni-i/belli, piccole mani, odorosi capelli', he finds himself singing, full voice. The majestic tenor sound rises effortlessly above the stave and down again through one of the most mellifluous phrases in the entire opera. Then, he breaks off, laughs impishly and almost apologetically, looks around at an appreciative orchestra, and gets back to his work as maestro.

Domingo has lived with this music for over thirty years now. Indeed, he may fairly claim to know this particular duet better than any other human being alive. Not only has he sung the tenor part in all the great opera houses of the world and conducted the opera at the Met and elsewhere, but, in a memorable and moving moment at a Met gala in 1991, he agreed to sing the *baritone* part in the Act IV duet opposite Pavarotti.

La Bohème is a musical and dramatic masterpiece. Musically, it is constructed in some ways like a symphony, with a longish first Act (or movement) laying out the basic themes, a boisterous *scherzo* (playful or vigorous movement) as Act II (the scene at the Café Momus), a slower, darker third Act, and a final Act in which much of the earlier material is reprised and resolved. The outer two Acts begin with the same rapid and syncopated descending figure representing the bohemians, while the inner two both begin with regular descending quaver chords — fast and brassy in Act II, cold and empty in Act III. In fact, many of the principal themes in the opera derive from the three- or four-note descending configurations that characterize the opening of each Act. Both Rodolfo and Mimì have a big, introductory showpiece to sing in Act I, and each is required to take a big breath in mid-aria and conquer their beloved, and the audience, with a long, *legato* phrase of descent (Rodolfo on the words 'Talor dal mio forziere', Mimì on 'Ma quando vien lo sgelo'). This subtle sense of musical consistency is intensified by the fact that both arias are filled with phrases that conclude with a sigh — a verbal 'feminine' ending and a musical drop of a fifth: '. . . come vivo, vuole', sings Rodolfo, dropping a fifth each time, and he does the same as he goes on to apostrophize Mimì's 'ochi belli', her beautiful eyes. They call me Mimì, she responds, but my real name is Lucia (drop of a fifth). I make artificial flowers — lilies and roses, 'gigli e rose' (drop of a fifth), which give me dreams known only to poetry, 'poesia' (drop of a fifth).

Dramatically, *Bohème* is an opera of pathos, a story of youngsters who tend to be on the receiving end of circumstances, victims of events beyond their control. These are not the movers and shakers of Verdi, the kings and queens for whom droopy, 'feminine' endings would normally be utterly inappropriate, not the passionate exotics of Puccini's own later works like *Tosca*, *Butterfly* or *Turandot*. No. The characters in *La Bohème* are simple, vulnerable folk in their early twenties with a naive and optimistic view of a world that is sometimes joyful and often cruel, who, like poor students everywhere, resort to exuberant high-jinks, passionate romance or extravagant rhetoric, perhaps to help mask the ordinariness of their lives. Marcello is painting 'The Red Sea' and wants to drown Pharaoh in it. Rodolfo, agreeing to burn the play he is writing to keep the fire alight, cries out that heroic measures are required when Rome is in peril. Their philosopher friend, Colline, asserts that the Apocalypse must be imminent as the pawn shops are shut.

La Bohème is more economically constructed, better controlled than Puccini's previous operas. There are no real loose ends (though one might wonder if and how Rodolfo returns Mimì's door key, which he pockets at the end of Act I, or whether the lovers do or do not stay together for a while after the end of Act III). Scene-setting at the beginning of each Act is masterly; the evocation of chilly dawn early in Act III is almost filmic in atmosphere and on a par with the warmer, Roman dawn that launches the last Act of *Tosca*. At the end of Act III of *La Bohème*, in one of the most miraculous sections of the score, the two central couples conduct two utterly different, though equally intense, conversations at the same time — Mimì and Rodolfo agreeing with infinite sadness that their love, though profound, will not last, while Musetta and Marcello act out an archetypal lovers' tiff and yell insults at each other. In the final Act, shortly after the opening duet, the four young men (and in Ross' production some of their neighbours) are required to act out a series of mock dances in quick succession — a gavotte, a minuet, a 'pavanella', a Spanish fandango and a graceful quadrille. The pace of all this horseplay is fragmented, but, in general, gets faster and faster until it is suddenly interrupted by Musetta's arrival with the dying Mimì in a *coup de théâtre* that, however often one sees the piece, always comes as a shock. As for the actual moment of Mimì's death, it is all the more poignant for being virtually unremarked. It takes a few moments before we, and the actors on stage, can take in the awfulness of what has happened; only then does Puccini permit his full orchestra to thunder out the final, falling phrases of the opera.

La Bohème provides many traps for the unwary conductor, as Domingo is the first to concede: 'One of the best compliments I ever had was in a review of my conducting of *Bohème*,' Domingo likes to recall. 'This critic said: "Domingo conducted *La Bohème* very well—but, after all, that's an easy opera to take on". Well,' he smiles, 'I'm glad he thinks it's an easy opera and that I made it *sound* easy to conduct, but, believe me, it really isn't. It's one of the most complicated!' It is also one of the most popular, he adds ruefully, so that all the people in the audience think *they* know exactly how the music should be performed.

Domingo is serious about his conducting and feels that his natural talent for it was nurtured by experiences in boyhood. 'I was brought up in the musical theatre,' he explains, recalling that after his parents left Spain for Mexico, they ran their own successful *zarzuela* company. 'I was always backstage, singing along, playing the piano, helping rehearse the performers,' he says, and he went on to study at the Mexican National Conservatory where he remembers sitting in on conducting classes with Igor Markevitch. One of his fellow students there was Eduardo Mata, who went on to become Music Director of the Dallas Symphony.

'I think you have to be born a conductor,' Domingo says with some finality, faintly amused at the eyebrows such a statement, from him, are bound to raise. You can learn all sorts of technical skills, he adds, 'but the *feeling* of conducting has to be inside you, it's something nobody can teach you'. Singing, he goes on (as though to answer the obvious unasked question) is something you have to *learn*: 'I mean, I wasn't born a tenor. Indeed, at first, after my voice changed, I thought I was going to be a baritone. But conducting— that's a skill you either have or you don't'.

Domingo is not the first performer to aspire to the conductor's podium. Indeed, many major-league maestri began their musical careers as distinguished soloists—Daniel Barenboim and Vladimir Ashkenazy, for example, were (and are) outstanding pianists. Some conductors, like Solti, Previn or Tilson Thomas (piano), Maazel or Marriner (violin), or Rostropovich (cello) still play their instruments to the highest standards. One or two maestri started out as singers (for example, Roger Norrington), but few established singers have ever gone on to make the transition with real success.

Even an artist of such palpable musical intelligence and sensitivity as Dietrich Fischer-Dieskau proved somewhat ineffective on the podium. Thus, as so often in his career, Domingo is treading ground that is risky, exposed, and littered with warning signs.

Domingo has the additional problem that, precisely because he is so universally revered as a *singer*, some people find it hard to believe that he can also have serious talent in other branches of the profession. 'It's probably part of a deal with the management,' the sceptics used to say when it was first announced that he was to conduct at the Vienna State Opera, Covent Garden or the Metropolitan. 'They have to indulge the whims of their top stars and Domingo must have bargained that he'd sing what they wanted if they'd also let him conduct.'

The scepticism was inevitable, and predictable, and Domingo was anxious from the start to allay it as far as he could and establish himself as a *bona fide* conductor. It was in the early 1970s that he first began to think seriously about conducting, attracted by the idea, at that time still very much at the back of his mind, that there might be a subsidiary musical career awaiting once the great voice eventually left him. In 1972, he and baritone Sherrill Milnes made the 'Domingo Conducts Milnes! Milnes Conducts Domingo!' album for RCA. Then, the following year, Julius Rudel let Domingo take charge of some performances of *La Traviata* at the New York City Opera. 'Plácido handled it all with great charm and aplomb,' Rudel recalls, adding that, though he may have been a little raw in those days, the performances already had 'a certain *élan*', and singers and orchestra liked and respected Domingo because he was clearly so musical and thoroughly professional.

In the years since, Domingo has built up an impressive secondary career as a conductor with a repertoire that includes several operas by Verdi (*Attila*, *Macbeth*, *Il Trovatore*, *La Traviata*, *Rigoletto* and *La Forza del Destino*), Rossini's *Il Barbiere di Siviglia*, a number of French operas (among them *Carmen* and Gounod's *Roméo et Juliette*), and Puccini's *Madama Butterfly*, *Tosca*, and, of course, *La Bohème*. A number of these are works with which he is primarily associated as a singer, but for many years Domingo's calling card as a conductor was one in which he did not normally sing—that most popular of operettas, Johann Strauss' *Die Fledermaus*. In 1986, he conducted the work on disc for E M I and sang the tenor lead role of Alfred on his own recording.

'At least I can't complain about the tempi taken by the conductor,' he joked later, looking back on this 'double'. The tenor originally scheduled for the part of Alfred was José Carreras. When Carreras had to pull out, Domingo suggested other possibilities — Francisco Araiza, for example, or maybe Peter Dvorsky. Only when it became clear that no high-quality tenor was available did Domingo decide to step into the breach himself and, after recording the opera in its entirety without Alfred, went on to overdub the missing role. This must be a feat unparalleled in recording history — made all the more difficult by the fact that, in addition to singing the notes written for him by Strauss, Alfred is also expected to bounce in from time to time with verbal and musical *ad libs*, which in this instance include a ringing version of Otello's 'Esultate!'.

What impact does Domingo the singer have upon Domingo the conductor? He considers this for a moment, then stresses the importance he places upon phrasing and breath control. 'Also, I am perhaps a bit too nice with singers,' he says with just the faintest flicker of a smile.

What about the impact of his conducting upon his own singing? Doesn't he want, when working under an indifferent maestro, to jump from the stage to the pit and take over? No (a bigger smile this time). 'When I conduct, I conduct, and when I sing — perhaps I have more sympathy for what a conductor has to do than some singers!' He adds that he finds conducting far more tiring than singing and, when he is scheduled to do both, as here in Los Angeles, would much prefer to sing the night before having to conduct than vice versa.

Domingo tends to be an intensely physical conductor, enlisting his whole body in the process of communication. His beat is vigorous, somewhat curvilinear, more upbeat than down, perhaps held a little low for everyone's comfort, and involves more parallel exertion of body and arms (and less of wrist) than is perhaps ideal. Watch him closely and you may detect at the great musical climaxes the same resolute toss of the head, the same clenched fists and slightly buckled knees that characterize his performances on stage as a singer. For the musical impulses emanating from Domingo are essentially the same.

Conductors who have worked with Domingo as a singer pay tribute to the depth and range of his musicianship. 'It's a joy having him at the other end of the stick,' says Lorin Maazel, 'because he really knows what's happening and one can communicate through just eye signals or whatever what ordinarily would take months of rehearsal to get across.' 'A wonderful sense of musical timing,' adds Zubin Mehta; 'you always know that *he* knows where he is going in a phrase.' Sir Georg Solti says, 'Plácido has a gift for phrasing that borders on the miraculous.'

In the recording studio, Domingo's musical curiosity and sensitivity extend to the technical aspects of recording, the way the balance between sections of the orchestra and between orchestra and voices can be altered not only by conductor but by engineers, and how the instrumentation might be adjusted to ease recording of a difficult bridge passage or transposition. 'Plácido's a musician through and through, not "merely" a singer', several maestri emphasize.

One of the most outstanding examples of a soloist who has made the transition to conductor successfully is Daniel Barenboim, a friend and colleague of Domingo's since the 1960s. Several of Domingo's recordings of French works have been conducted by Barenboim. When they meet, they chat in Spanish (part of Barenboim's boyhood was spent in Argentina, part of Domingo's in Mexico). They have Israel in common, too—Barenboim spent his adolescence there, Domingo his early twenties. How good a conductor Domingo will eventually become Barenboim cannot say, nor how thoroughly he can read a complicated orchestral score, but he is impressed by the way Domingo as a singer clearly thinks orchestrally. 'A certain interest in orchestration and in conducting is very helpful to any musician because it forces him to hear everything with orchestral ears,' he says, and notes that Domingo always knows not only his own singing line but also much of what his colleagues have to sing, plus the instrumental colours, textures, and harmonies. 'Plácido plays the piano well and is far more aware than most singers of all that is going on under what he sings.' He adds a note of caution, however: 'Being outstandingly musical is not enough to make you into a good conductor. When you play or sing as a soloist, a large percentage of your performance depends upon your own musical

69

intuition. But when you conduct, you have to persuade others to play the way you hear the music in your head, and to do this you must be able to rationalize and analyse — and communicate to others — your own musical instincts.' Which is why, this former child prodigy adds, you can occasionally have a child prodigy pianist or violinist, but never a real child prodigy conductor.

Does Domingo have this capacity to analyse and communicate his musical instincts or is he, on the podium, ultimately no more than a talented amateur? Domingo himself acknowledges at once that, of course, his singing has to take priority and that he has a long way to go before he will approach similar proficiency as a conductor. However, he speaks with enthusiasm about those conducting classes by Markevitch in Mexico, and about practical lessons he has learned from admired colleagues, ranging from Nello Santi to Carlos Kleiber, and he can become quite earnest about his own aspirations. He can also be very funny. I once asked him whether he thought conducting opera was easier than taking on the symphonic repertoire (he can turn out a spiritedly rhythmical account of Beethoven's Seventh); after all, opera was, in general, already more familiar to him. True, he acknowledged, but, when you conduct opera, you've got two sets of forces to control at once, the singers 'upstairs' and the players 'downstairs'. 'It's like being a Roman gladiator,' he laughed, finding a metaphor he has often used since, and throwing his limbs precariously in all directions to illustrate the point — 'You've got one leg in one chariot pulled by a hundred horses in one direction, and the other in another chariot pulled by another hundred horses in a different direction!' The sheer effort involved in keeping all those horses under control is one of the hardest jobs an operatic conductor is called upon to do. If he fails, he will be torn apart by the various powerful forces nominally at his command. If he succeeds, he will have the chance to preside over one of those glorious, multifaceted musical ensembles that constitute opera at its grandest.

'*Bambam bambam bambam bam-ba-ba bam-ba-ba bambam bambam bambam bam-ba-ba bam-ba-ba bam . . .*'

Plácido Domingo, face and neck muscles tense, is mouthing the brisk, highly accented trumpet rhythms that open Act II of *La Bohème*. It is faster than the players expect and they are in danger of falling over each other as they catch up with the *Allegro focoso* Domingo wishes to sustain. Not only must the tempo be established from the first chord, but the sound must be a little more brash and brassy. This is a street scene, almost a fairground scene — the sharpest possible contrast to the ethereal love duet that ended the previous Act.

'Aranci, datteri, ninnoli!
Caldi marroni e caramelle!'

They are selling everything on the streets of Paris this Christmas Eve — oranges, dates, plums, hot chestnuts, chocolate milk, every kind of fruit, flowers, sweets and sweetmeats. There are children on the lookout for toys, mothers on the lookout for children, young men looking for girls, young women keen to be found. As the brassy chords erupt from the pit, Ross has the entire chorus ranged right across the front of the stage before a colourful drop curtain, selling their wares at top volume. One of the 'bohemians' is briefly seen and heard haggling over a musical instrument; another buys a coat. The drop curtain rises and the chorus merge naturally into the crowded streets around the Café Momus, mingling with the waiters, shoppers and hucksters already circulating there. The score moves, cinematically, from crowd scene to close-up. Rodolfo buys Mimì a pink bonnet and introduces her to his friends. A toyseller touts his wares. Meanwhile, the whole time, the busy crowd surges back and forth, every nuance highlighted by Puccini's quicksilver score. This is music theatre at its most magical, but there are an awful lot of 'horses' for the man in the pit to control, and if the scene is to work well and remain fluid it will call upon all of Ross' great experience as both choreographer and film maker.

Ross' intention is to make every person on stage an individual 'character'. In earlier production rehearsals, he would line them up in front of the drop curtain for the opening of Act II, scrutinize them from the production desk in the middle of the orchestra stalls, and address them through a microphone: 'Is that a baby you are carrying? Yes, you. Is that supposed to be a baby? It looks like a dirty towel. It must look like a human being. Somebody who is used to carrying a baby show him how to carry a baby!'

Ross has a way of repeating certain words and phrases, perhaps to reinforce the point he is making: 'The lady in the polka-dot dress. No, not you, the lady in the polka-dot dress next to the two weightlifters. Yes. Move to your right. Do you see that space to your right? Yes. Well, fill that space. Further. Right. Stop. Everybody: if you see a space, fill it. I don't want to see any unfilled spaces.'

The chorus consists predominantly of members of the Los Angeles Master Chorale, inheritor of the mantle of the famous Roger Wagner Chorale. They (like the Los Angeles Chamber Orchestra) are hired in by the Los Angeles Opera to participate in particular productions, and many members express astonishment at the thoroughness and detail with which Ross rehearses them. 'Most opera directors just give us the most general instructions,' one confides, and says that with Ross it is as though he is choreographing every single frame of a complicated feature film. 'It's wonderful being observed so precisely,' says another, who has never been cast as an individual 'character' before, 'but it's also dangerous. You never known when you're going to be the one he picks on!'

'O K . Go back to your "Ah" positions,' calls Ross over the microphone. Everyone on stage spools back to the freeze-frame moment where they all sing 'Ah' just before Mimì curtseys before a wealthy aristocrat she encounters and arouses Rodolfo's first tiny pang of jealousy. This is one of the many deft touches added by Ross (derived from Murger) to help fill out the details of Puccini's libretto. If Rodolfo later on complains that Mimì is a flirt, and Musetta in Act I V mentions that Mimì has left her 'Viscontino', why not introduce the Viscontino as a silent presence earlier in the opera?

Ross is treating *Bohème* as a serious drama. At his first rehearsal, he took the unusual step of sitting all his principal singers around a table for a complete read-through of the English translation of the text. There are some operas you couldn't do that with, he says, 'but *Bohème* reads well as a drama and we all learned a lot from the exercise.' As a result, everyone knows everything that happens in the opera, including what happens during those scenes when they themselves are offstage.

'I wanted to treat *La Bohème* not as a venerated masterpiece,' Ross says, 'though it is that of course, but as though it had only just been written and we were all coming to it for the first time.' Perhaps partly for this reason, he and his designer Gerard Howland have placed the action not in the 1830s or 1840s but at the end of the century, when Puccini wrote it. We see the Paris of the Impressionists, of the almost completed Eiffel Tower, of Mallarmé, Zola, and the young Satie and Debussy. True, the Eiffel Tower was completed in 1889, the centenary of the French Revolution, while the motor car in which they have Musetta arrive in Act II looks vintage *c.* 1908. Purists might object to a *fin de siècle* setting of a libretto sprinkled with references to King Louis Philippe and Prime Minister Guizot, but a broadly consistent sense of period is richly evoked. Musetta, for example — played with smouldering sensuality by the Odessa-born Israeli soprano Tatyana Odinokova in orange wig and dress, long necklace, turquoise choker and long black gloves — looks the very embodiment of a Toulouse-Lautrec painting.

Then, there are the details Ross has added: Mimì, lonely and frail, dropping her basket of flowers and slowly climbing the rickety stairs to her room at the very beginning of the opera, aware of the attractive young men who are her neighbours; the landlord Benoit, who is rude about skinny women, revealed as a henpecked husband with a thin, bossy wife; and Mimì's suave Viscontino, a shadowy character who appears again at the beginning and end of Act III before he is finally mentioned in the text in Act IV.

Ross is sensitive, too, to the passage of time. In the first three Acts, snowdrifts huddle alongside the buildings; in the fourth it is spring, and the bleak rooftops-and-chimneys world of Act I now reappears, but is garlanded with flowers as the whole neighbourhood comes alive with activity. Mimì is placed in a sun chair in the roof garden — perfect for an 1890s tuberculosis patient — where Rodolfo tells her she is 'bella come un aurora' before she expires.

This is a big production, ambitious, fresh, re-thought. Howland's designs are huge and evocative, filling the cavernous Dorothy Chandler stage with lovingly recreated chunks of *fin de siècle* Paris. Rarely can an operatic production have required so many props — and not just the key and candle, the bonnet, pen and paintbrush, muff and medicines required by the text. One day, backstage, I encountered a woman in a headscarf and long dress brandishing a pair of curved iron constructions. 'Those look menacing,' I said, feigning fear; 'sure — they're for beating the hell out of carpets at the beginning of Act IV,' she laughed. The second Act alone would break the bank and storage space available to most prop shops: all those oranges and plums, cookies and sweetmeats for the opening chorus; dumbbells for Ross' hoax weightlifters; a silver-topped cane for the Viscontino and flowers for him to offer Mimì; an array of magic tricks for the toyseller, Parpignol; expensive packing cases for Musetta to unload from the automobile in which she arrives; a cigar for Marcello to chomp on; and a French tricolor flag for virtually everyone on stage to wave as a band of black zouaves swagger their way through the march that ends the Act.

It is early September and Plácido Domingo is up in Rehearsal Room 3 with his *Bohème* principals and a pianist. He has just come from a staging rehearsal for *Ballo* in another of the upstairs rooms. Before him are seated his four bohemians, plus Benoit and Mimì. Most have little plastic bottles of mineral water ritualistically placed beneath their chairs. The auditorium itself is given over today to final technical and lighting rehearsals for *La Bohème*, while the orchestra is working on *Ballo* in the Grand Hall, in the front of house. The gala opening is a week away and there is a lot of opera going on in the Dorothy Chandler Pavilion today. This is the last chance for Domingo and his singers to work together in an intimate atmosphere and go through some of the details of Puccini's score.

'Nei cieli bigi guardo fumar dai mille comignoli Parigi', sings Craig Sirianni — Rodolfo's very first phrase and an important precursor of the big aria that will come later in Act I. Sirianni, with his colourful Hawaiian shirt, fashionably baggy trousers and hair in a pony tail, is still in the early stages of a highly promising career. One day he turned up for rehearsal but reported that he had a high temperature: 'Great!,' quipped LA Opera's resident conductor Randall Behr, 'just what the world's waiting for — the latest hot young tenor!'

Today, though, Sirianni is in excellent health and voice, and if he has any qualms about singing before the man conducting him, he shows no sign of them. Equally, Domingo, beating time conscientiously with a pencil, does not betray any sense of having special vocal prowess when he is dealing with the singers. If he is inclined to illustrate anything to them, it is how to convey the meaning of the language they are singing in the best way possible. 'L'uno brucia in un soffio', for example, can be quicker, he suggests to Sirianni, for the phrase means 'it burns in a flash'. 'Soffio', they sing to each other, trying to use the little grace note that Puccini has written to catch the spirit behind the word. Domingo insists that double consonants be properly pronounced ('Luigi Filippo', 'Ed ora come faccio', 'che viso d'ammalata') — 'particularly when there's no orchestra playing. You never know, there might be someone out there in the audience who knows Italian!'

They reach the great tenor aria, 'Che gelida manina', and Sirianni launches in. 'Whenever you want, Craig,' says Plácido matter-of-factly, 'you can take your time. I'll just beat the opening note, and you can come in whenever you are ready.' Sirianni does so. 'But don't break up the phrase. Just let it flow forwards to the next phrase, as if you were a young man of twenty, say, just talking to this girl.'

Plácido pauses for a moment: 'You know, I'm fifty-two and I still sing Rodolfo. You're — I don't know — twenty years younger than me or whatever. But we all have to *be* Rodolfo or Mimì or the rest, just young and fresh as they were, whoever we ourselves might be . . .' Pause. Everyone senses that this is an important moment as Domingo, in effect, reaches out across a generation to touch his young colleagues, to enter their world and perhaps help draw them into his.

However, there's little time at rehearsals for sentiment. Domingo picks up his pencil again and looks at his score. 'The thing is this. You're playing — what? — more or less teenagers. And when you think of the way they live, well, it mustn't be melancholic, the tempo must really flow. So. These opening phrases of the aria, don't think of individual words so much as where each phrase is going.'

Domingo is keen to pass on whatever he can of his own experience as a singer to this younger generation ('especially of course to a tenor!'), but is adamant that his own unrivalled expertise does not make him want to join the martinet school of maestri. 'It's not that I try to say to Craig "sing it like this because this is the way I sing it". Not at all. Rather, it's a question of feeling, style, phrasing, expression, use of *legato* — everything that is involved in singing.'

Sirianni goes for the aria again and the whole thing flows beautifully. His phrasing is not identical to that which Domingo adopts when *he* sings this piece — Domingo, for example, often tends to move in more quickly on the impatient words 'Aspetti signorina . . .' But Sirianni's shaping of the aria is just as valid and Domingo as conductor is happy to follow him.

All the members of the cast notice how sensitive Domingo is to their phrasing: 'He really is sympathetic towards the singer,' says Esperian appreciatively, 'because, being a singer himself, he knows all the pitfalls. For example, if you have a really long phrase, he's not going to drag it out because he knows exactly when you have to breathe and, if necessary, he'll instinctively speed things up.' However, she adds, it is not just the technical aspects of singing that inform Domingo's conducting. 'Plácido's also a great actor, and so he gives a lot of advice on how to use the words, for example, to fill out the character you're playing.' 'I think what gives Plácido the real edge is how much he understands the psychological game of playing opera,' adds Jeffrey Black. 'It's a bit like the psychological game of playing tennis — you know, when to push, when to draw back, when to be sympathetic. He just knows instinctively how to get the best out of us.'

Domingo was not able to be present at all the early piano sessions and much of the groundwork was done by Randall Behr (who is, in any case, to conduct later performances in the run). However, Domingo's presence seems to add an extra dimension, a further shot of adrenalin to a team of young artists keen to display their talents. It is this obvious sympathy between a great singer of one generation and his successors of the next that cements the bond between them. 'He has this capacity to identify with the singers the other end of the baton,' they all agree, 'and by no means every famous maestro has it. But Plácido, with all his experience as a singer, instinctively builds up the musical and dramatic textures around our needs and abilities. And for us, that's a wonderful feeling.'

That night, after a three-hour *Ballo* production rehearsal and then a four-hour *Bohème* rehearsal as conductor, Domingo has yet another appointment. He slips into a studio in town where he is recording the final tracks of an album of Latin American songs. He is in superb voice, as though physically and mentally refreshed by all those concentrated hours of work earlier in the day.

This is the regular pattern while Domingo is in Los Angeles. Each day he rehearses *Bohème*, *Ballo* or both. Between times, he might be recording his Latin American album, or brushing up Act I of *Die Walküre* or learning the title role of Verdi's *Stiffelio* (both of which are coming up shortly at the Metropolitan Opera, New York). Time has to be found, too, for various public appearances, each of which, in its own way, represents one of the magnets that has drawn Domingo back so often to Los Angeles. These include a press conference with L A M C O director Peter Hemmings and Ross to launch the new *Bohème*; a ceremony at which Domingo is honoured with a star on the Hollywood Walk of Fame; and a 'Viva Los Artistas' brunch celebrating the lifetime achievements of Domingo and three other top Latino performers.

All this constitutes a busy timetable, but it is not exceptional by Domingo's normal standards. For thirty years, people have commented on the ferocious schedule he consistently sets himself. Everyone who has worked with him has stories of how he jetted in to rehearse this or that opera in one place, disappeared to do a recording or T V appearance or, perhaps, a performance of a different opera somewhere else, perhaps a continent away (even, in one or two notorious instances, the other side of the Atlantic), and somehow was back, bright and breezy, when required a day later. In Vienna during early *Walküre* rehearsals, Domingo had to jet off twice in order to fulfil long-standing concert commitments in Poland and Finland. Here, in Los Angeles, his first orchestral run-through of *Bohème* was slotted in between a couple of performances of *Parsifal* in Bayreuth.

It is not only Domingo's punishing schedule of work that people remark upon, it is also his immense social energy. He can work a crowd with the unfailing affability of an American politician running for office, and clearly enjoys chatting easily in any of several languages to high and low alike. I have seen him talking with complete ease to the King and Queen of Spain on one occasion and to the cleaning ladies at Covent Garden on another — in the first case with respect, but no artificial reverence, in the second with simplicity, but not a whiff of condescension. He is helped by a prodigious memory that seems to have space not only for all the roles he performs and the minutiae of a complicated schedule, but also for the charming trivia of social life. He recalls who everybody is (or pretends convincingly to do so), is good at names, and does not let any friend go untouched or unaddressed. I remember meeting him some weeks after one of his opening nights at Covent Garden in the mid-1980s and being astonished when he asked why he hadn't seen me at the party after that particular show. A month after a Vienna *Lohengrin* in 1990, he said he had spotted me standing in the Staatsoper audience during the final ovation, told me precisely where I was, and asked why I hadn't come backstage afterwards (there was a good reason; I knew he was leaving Vienna at six the next morning to fly to London to catch Concorde to New York, thence down to San Juan for a performance of *Otello*).

Opera lore abounds with jokes about stupid tenors, and Domingo is not above making one or two himself: 'Plácido,' said James Levine one night, coming round to compliment Domingo after a performance of *Tosca*, 'you were great. You know, you really have the mind of a conductor.' Domingo smiled into his dressing room mirror and shot back the comment: 'Thanks Jimmy, but it's just as well that you don't have the mind of a tenor!' Domingo's conversation can be rather like the game of a good tennis partner: he will adjust his play to yours so that rallies are as fulfilling or as demanding as you wish them to be. 'For a tenor you're quite a big fellow,' said one female colleague provocatively during a break in rehearsals, and Domingo replied with a grin, 'You mean, for a big fellow I'm quite a tenor!'

This versatile and voluble sociability seems to constitute a central feature of Domingo's make-up. It appears important to him that he should always have someone to talk to, something or someone to engage with. He is very bad at sitting around with nothing to do, and it is impossible to imagine Domingo remaining alone at the edge of a crowd absorbed in a book. If there is no crowd, Domingo will seek and make one; if there is, he will assuredly be in the middle of it. If ever there was a man of action, this is it, a person whose jaw or fingers or leg will tremble if he has to suffer enforced immobility, even for a matter of minutes. During stage rehearsals for *Bohème* in Los Angeles, Domingo could often be seen at the conductor's rostrum twitching his baton like a water diviner until his contribution to the proceedings was required again.

It is simply resorting to cliché, however, to say that Domingo's work schedule and relentless sociability are forms of neurotic hyperactivity that compensate for deep inner uncertainties or that he has a stronger need to be loved than the rest of us. The personal style of the man has nothing of frenetic insecurity about it; on the contrary, Domingo comes across as a man of considerable inner strength and certainty whose non-stop activity when in public arises out of genuine relish for all he does rather than from any sense of inner self-doubt. When I asked him once if he was a workaholic, he gently brushed the question aside and said, with transparent sincerity, that he simply loves what he does and seems to thrive on doing it. If his instincts prove so fruitful, he was saying, in effect, why not follow them?

There is clearly a link between the style of the man and the career of the artist. Just as every friend's hand is regularly shaken or cheek kissed, Domingo also makes a point of visiting most of the world's major opera houses, and several of the minor ones, each season, and new Domingo recordings continue to flow from several different record companies. 'He has a deep inner need to get everybody's vote,' says someone who has known him well for many years, so he will 'leave no friend or opera house or impresario or colleague or record company too long without a new gesture of trust and friendship.' All of which is fine in itself, adds the friend; 'but wanting to say yes to everybody, he often lands up having to make most of them wait as a result.'

Everyone who has dealt with Domingo has a story to illustrate the point: how it took Domingo years to fulfil a promise to make this recording, give that interview, perform in such-and-such a city. I remember the problems Domingo had even finding time to work on his own autobiography, *My First Forty Years*, with his patient ghost writer, Harvey Sachs. 'If I don't get on with it soon,' Domingo would quip guiltily, 'it will have to be retitled *My First Fifty Years!*'

One day in Domingo's dressing room at La Scala, Milan, Sachs tactfully pressed Plácido on when they could get together to tape the final sections of the book. It could all be wrapped up in about three days. By now Domingo was feeling terrible about having kept Sachs waiting for so long. 'O K,' he said eventually, glancing at Marta for approval, 'why don't you come to Barcelona for Christmas, Harvey? We can surely have our three years then!' Everyone fell about at the Freudian slip. Domingo may have meant three *days*, but he often keeps people waiting for *years*.

People are always accusing Domingo of jetting around too much and undertaking too much work. The contention is perhaps exaggerated, but not without foundation. By his early fifties, Domingo had given close to 2500 performances, sung over 100 roles and recorded far and away the largest operatic discography of any tenor in history. Does he really do 'too much', though, and if so, what would constitute 'enough'?

Domingo certainly travels incessantly and only tends to stop for long in one place if a really substantial work commitment requires him to do so. During rehearsals for *Il Guarany* in Bonn in 1994, his diary showed him conducting performances of *I Puritani* in Vienna and singing *Carmen* in London and *Tosca* in Paris (see pp. 160–61). Caruso was not able to do this sort of thing, of course, and would spend many months at a time every year based in New York. He may have made the occasional trip up or down the north-east coast of the USA to do a performance in Philadelphia, say, or a recording in nearby Camden, New Jersey, but the thought of spending thirty-six hours in Mexico City or Puerto Rico between performances at the Met would have been beyond his comprehension. To Domingo, however, this sort of excursion is perfectly normal.

Look, though, at the performance schedule Caruso was prepared to set himself. For example, in his first London season, in the spring of 1902, Caruso sang twenty-four performances of eight different operas in two and a half months. Giulio Gatti-Casazza records that, in his first week as Director of the New York Metropolitan Opera in 1908, his star tenor sang in *Faust* (at the newly opened Brooklyn Academy of Music), *Aida* at the Met, *Bohème* in Philadelphia, then *Butterfly*, *Traviata* and *Tosca* at the Met—six performances of six different roles in three theatres in just eight days. Caruso travelled widely, too. In an era when travel took time, he appeared in Italy, Russia, Germany, France, Belgium, Portugal, Spain, Monaco, Austria, Hungary, Czechoslovakia, England, Ireland, Scotland, Argentina, Brazil, Uruguay, Mexico, Cuba, Canada, and, of course, the United States. At the Met alone, in 18 years he gave over 600 performances.

Let us try to put this into finer focus. However hard any singer might work, this does not compare with the performance schedule undertaken by a busy instrumentalist. A singer uses his instrument as he talks, and if he is physically below par, so is his instrument. If he uses it one day, it will inevitably be more tired the next. A pianist, however, can perform every day with substantially less physical wear and tear. There may be mental strain, of course, and a tired pianist, violinist or whoever will not play as well as a relaxed, refreshed one. But a Paderewski or a Pachmann, a Rubinstein or Heifetz, Stern or Brendel, can notch up a string of performances — twenty or more during a one-month tour of the United States or Europe — that not even the most energetic singer could match. Furthermore, Domingo, unlike some other leading opera singers, does not give *Lieder* recitals, for example, or evenings of arias with piano accompaniment. His occasional concerts — usually with orchestra and at least one other singer — are often massively promoted, but only incidental to the main thrust of his career. Therefore, by the standards of the busy opera singer who also has a thriving concert career, Domingo might almost be considered to be working at a merely modest rate!

Domingo himself, when asked about the amount of work he takes on, adds, not unreasonably, that everything he does tends to be very visible, much reported, and therefore people *think* he performs more often than others whereas, in fact, his schedule is not dissimilar to that of other leading opera singers. Furthermore, he is able to teach himself most of his own roles at the piano so that (except for something unusually demanding like Siegmund in *Die Walküre*) he feels he does not need to spend time going to coaching sessions like most other singers. Domingo has a quick and retentive mind and knows he can normally master the details of a new production of a familiar work in just one or two rehearsals. Many times I have known him turn up towards the end of a rehearsal period, much to the unspoken resentment of colleagues who may already have been hard at work for two or three weeks, and slot easily into their production, bringing it huge added lustre on the night. In all these ways, Domingo insists he actually takes on *less* work than some in his profession.

However, consider what he chooses to do with the time 'saved'. There is that phenomenal discography, with many complete operas now recorded up to four times, the films (*Traviata*, *Cav* and *Pag*, *Carmen*, *Otello*), television appearances and concerts and, nowadays, his regular commitments as a conductor. Above all, there are his periodic feats of artistic bravado, such as his participation in the 1990 'Three Tenors' concert (where each solo piece he sang was in a different language and from a different musical style), the reunion concert in 1994, or the live telecast of *Tosca* from the authentic locations in Rome at the times of day and night specified in the score, including Act III looking out over an authentic Roman dawn. In June 1993, in Vienna for Siegmund once more, this time as part of the complete *Ring* cycle, Domingo also sang the part of Luigi in Puccini's one-act opera *Il Tabarro* at the Volksoper and then took a well-publicized tram trip across town to the Staatsoper just in time to go on as Canio in *I Pagliacci*.

Does all this constitute 'too much'? The only realistic criterion by which an artist's schedule can be appraised is whether he delivers what he promises. Some take on what would seem to be a reasonably light workload yet still fail to deliver; the seductive road to operatic stardom is littered with the bones of singers who, often for temperamental as much as vocal reasons, fell by the wayside. Others, however, like to assume a load that would overwhelm most people yet delight in it. Domingo does take on a great deal of work and routinely intersperses his public commitments with many other demands on his time, energies, and talents, yet he seems to thrive on this kind of life, continues to turn in performances and recordings of outstanding quality, and is capable of total relaxation when appropriate. He can sleep on planes and I have seen him cat-nap during car trips and awaken fully refreshed. Domingo works hard, in other words, not because he is (as one concerned friend put it) riding a tiger and scared to get off, but because he knows life suits him best this way. He is like a rechargeable battery, as another experienced

Domingo-watcher phrased it, because all the activity he demands of himself appears not to wear him out, but, rather, to give to him renewed energy. A cushion cover in his New York apartment is tellingly embossed with the motto: 'IF I REST I RUST'.

Colleagues have always joked about Domingo's non-stop work habits. The great Swedish soprano Birgit Nilsson once said affectionately that among Domingo's many talents he is also a brilliant linguist, 'but, alas, he has not yet learned to say "no" in any language!' Domingo adores Nilsson but it irritates him that this comment is so frequently quoted. 'Look,' he says emphatically, 'it is not that I *cannot* say no. It's that I feel I have no need to. I know people say this about me out of affection and concern, but they need not worry. If anybody knows and cares about my career and my voice, it is me!' Also, although everybody complains about how hard he pushes himself, they really want it that way. 'Nobody ever says to me: "OK, Plácido, don't come to us, you'll tire yourself and do yourself harm".' The very people who accuse him of taking on too much work, he feels, are often precisely the ones who are collectively responsible for it.

This pattern goes back to the earliest days of his career; there are still people in the music world in Israel, for example, who talk with awe of Domingo singing one night in three for two-and-a-half years during his stint there in the early 1960s. 'Even then they told me I was doing too much and would ruin my voice!' he recalls. After Israel, he systematically undertook a series of auditions in the major houses of Europe and, by the time he was giving his débuts in them a few years later, he was already retaining the services of a publicity agent in several locations. Domingo, a naturally outgoing and generous man, would often throw a backstage party or take the cast out for dinner to mark his birthday or each time his number of performances reached a new, significant figure. Rather like a good politician, he would assiduously keep in touch with friends and colleagues by means of carefully placed phone calls, flowers, telegrams or gifts of one sort or another. In much the same way, he would be sure to schedule at least a few performances every season in half-a-dozen or more countries and, in recent years, has made sure that he would be seen conducting regularly. In addition, there have been periodic press interviews in each country, occasional

high-visibility concert appearances, record-signing sessions and so
on. All these elements of Domingo's behaviour paint a picture of a
personality that, in some ways, is akin to that of a chairman of a big,
multinational corporation who is keen to keep an eye on all the
subsidiary companies, or a general who is anxious to keep his far-
flung troops in line. As Domingo's schedule has not been that of an
artist forced to accept whatever work he can manage to get, this
pattern of keeping the entire circuit assiduously well watered, so to
speak, must have been one of his own choosing. This is a man who
likes to try to keep everybody happy.

The ambition, the insatiable appetite for work have clearly been
present throughout his career. So has the desire to please. Domingo
has a reputation — in a profession notorious for backbiting — for
being exceptionally courteous and helpful towards colleagues. One
soprano recalls a time when she was rehearsing a performance that
was to be televized and the gentle way Domingo helped show her
how to play to the cameras more effectively. Another remembers
how he helped direct her towards a repertoire more appropriate for
her voice. A third singer, who was having troubles with an agent,
took up Domingo's recommendation of another agent and has been
glad about this decision ever since. The American soprano Leona
Mitchell (who was to sing Amelia to Domingo's Gustavo in the Los
Angeles production of *Ballo*) told me many years ago how grateful
she was when Domingo, already one of the great stars of opera,
made her feel part of the team when she made her début at the New
York Metropolitan as Micaëla in *Carmen* in 1976 at the age of twenty-
four. Film director John Schlesinger, though very accomplished in
his usual field, was a novice to operatic production when he directed
Domingo in *Hoffmann* at Covent Garden in 1980, and he told me
that Domingo was a tower of strength. 'He virtually held my hand
in early rehearsals, yet was quite prepared to take direction as
though he had never sung the role before.' Even fellow tenors speak
warmly of Domingo's kindness. One, who took over a run of
*Traviata*s from Domingo at the Met in 1981, told me of the immense
practical help Domingo gave him when they discussed details of the
role of Alfredo. 'Competitive? Yes, he is,' another singer agreed,
'but only with himself. It's his *own* artistic achievement, not anyone
else's, that he always wants to improve upon.'

Domingo's innate courtesy and openness extend to strangers. When I first got to know him, I was astonished how candid he would be about various possible projects, some of which were still subject to delicate negotiations. When I asked about details of past performances, he lent me his private diaries. Most people in the public eye would be more reserved about what they revealed to someone they scarcely knew. How, I wondered then and have often wondered since, can so obviously ambitious and work-driven a man appear at the same time so relaxed, helpful, generous, and trusting? Was he as open with others who came to interview him as he was with me and, if so, had not some abused his trust? The answer to both these questions, I later came to know, was 'yes'. Inevitably, inaccurate or indiscreet things have been printed about him from time to time—any rich, handsome and talented international celebrity is bound to be misrepresented in the press in this way. However, it is precisely because Domingo is so open, that he sometimes tells friends and journalists more than he probably should.

So we have a happy worker and compulsive glad-hander, competitive yet trusting, ambitious yet a generous team player, a brilliant performer in public yet prepared to be revealingly frank in private conversation; the successful integration of all these qualities in one person would seem almost too good to be true. Indeed, journalists looking for a story have sometimes found Domingo too much of a paragon to be really 'interesting'. Doesn't he have faults, they would ask? What about his private life and all those beautiful women who pursue him? How much does he earn and what tax does he pay? What about contracts he has broken? What gets him really angry? What about that alleged birth date of 1941— surely he is lying about his age? What does he *really* think about Pavarotti?

The hounds of the press were barking up a forest of wrong trees if they thought they would penetrate to the inner 'truth' about Domingo with this kind of approach. For Domingo, although open and frank in his personal and professional dealings, gradually learned, with the advent of ever greater celebrity, to protect himself from intrusive demands upon his time and attention, and to develop greater single-mindedness, an ability to focus on the main task and

85

to cut out more and more of the peripheral activities (and perhaps see less of the peripherati who used to feel they had automatic rights of access). Courtesy and courtliness can charm; he learned that they could also be used to exclude.

Domingo acknowledges that there was a shift of attitude and is inclined to date it from around the time of the Mexican earthquake of 1985 in which relatives of his were killed, and the death of his father not long afterwards, two events that, naturally, affected him profoundly. 'I was touched by tragedy, by loss,' he reflects, 'and I think as a result my priorities shifted.'

These events were followed by a particularly stressful period in his professional life (including a series of minor illnesses and highly publicized cancellations), and a gradual change of direction. His conversation at the time tended to turn increasingly back to his Hispanic roots — to Spain, Mexico, Latin America. This is the period when the Los Angeles Opera was founded and Domingo agreed to become Artistic Consultant from the outset as a token of his dedication to the huge Hispanic presence in Southern California. Then plans were finalized for the new Maestranza Opera in Seville and here, too, Domingo agreed to act as Artistic Adviser (a role that was to assume major proportions when Seville played host to 'Expo '92'). In 1986, he starred in the world première of Menotti's *Goya*, a work written specifically for him and which (despite the reservations of critics) gave Domingo and the Chilean soprano Victoria Vergara some attractively singable music, as well as a splendidly Spanish theme. It was in the middle and late 1980s, too, that he returned to the music of his youth and found time to appear with Spanish *zarzuela* companies in the United States and elsewhere. In the summer of 1988, Domingo fulfilled a long-held dream: he presented a concert to the people of New York on the Great Lawn of Central Park in which he was joined by Rosario Andrade, Gloria Estefan and Linda Ronstadt for a programme that culminated in a series of *zarzuela* and *mariachi* numbers which sent the audience home afterwards walking on air.

Above all, there was the shadow of Mexico. As the memory of the disastrous earthquake receded, Domingo continued to identify himself with a series of charitable projects: a village for 200 families, complete with its own kindergarten, clinic and social facilities; two houses for earthquake orphans; and a facility, supervised by Father Gonzalez Torres, whereby every penny raised for Domingo projects would be doubled by the Mexican Government.

As Domingo's personal priorities shifted, there was a corresponding development in his artistry, a more inward-looking quality than before, a perceptible interiorization of emotion, an intensity of utterance and movement that was the greater for being more economical. Hence, perhaps, his evident desire to add to his repertoire the heavier, more demanding roles more appropriate to his years and increasing maturity. Throughout this period he still managed to retain much of the youthful ardour required for works like *Fanciulla*, *Bohème* or *Ballo*, and I remember, for example, being riveted by the sunny intensity of his entrance aria, 'Amor ti vieta', in a performance before a Spanish audience of Giordano's *Fedora*. Artistically, however, the most memorable feature of these years was the way Domingo seemed to discover greater depth than ever before in parts like Otello, Canio and Lohengrin, and found himself increasingly drawn towards the heavier, German repertoire. They were the years, too, when his young colleague and compatriot José Carreras nearly died of leukemia, an event so shocking that it helped cause the two of them, as well as the Italian tenor Luciano Pavarotti, to bury years of sharpened hatchets and eventually to appear in public together in a concert that, in a single night, did all three of them more good than had been achieved by years of unacknowledged rivalry.

Perhaps it would be foolish to talk of a 'new' Domingo. The energy, the quiet concentration in rehearsal, the intense commitment in performance and the charm after the show — these qualities were all present in abundance in the 1990s, the 1980s and 1970s. Something had changed, however, in Domingo's bearing, both on and off the stage. He says he values his privacy and time with his family, especially Marta, more than ever before, and tends now to accept only the engagements he really wants, turning down other time-consuming invitations. 'One day,' Plácido told me, 'Marta and I arrived back in New York after four months away and there was a huge pile of invitations to do this and that and the other. And Marta said, very wisely, "Plácido. New York is still here and they have all managed wonderfully without us. So they can manage

87

without us just as well for the next two months, even though we happen to be here!".'

By the 1990s, Domingo had become appreciably less available to the press, wondering with a touch of genuine bewilderment why journalists always wanted to come to ask him the same questions: 'People always accused me of saying "Yes" to everything [his brow furrowing deeply — shades of that infamous quote from Nilsson]. Well, I'm sorry if people don't like it, but maybe at last I have learned to say "No".'

Perhaps what we are observing is simply the process of ageing, of maturing, of a man who has reached the pinnacle of one of the world's most demanding and difficult professions and, in the years remaining to him, wants to sharpen the focus of what he aims to achieve. With the prospect of more *Otello*, *Pagliacci* and Wagner, but probably no *Traviata*, *Rigoletto* or *Manon Lescaut*, Domingo seems set to continue to shift his centre of gravity towards the darker, more mature timbres of his voice and artistic personality. He has talked from time to time about singing Beethoven's *Fidelio*, Britten's *Peter Grimes*, Tchaikovsky's *Pique Dame*, and — the one the entire operatic world has been waiting for — Wagner's *Tristan und Isolde* (now scheduled for 1996). In general, Domingo is likely to continue to solidify and refine his existing operatic repertoire, add to the range of his recordings, systematically extend his experience as a conductor and take up the reins as Artistic Director of Washington Opera (from 1996), as he gradually moves inexorably towards the eventual end of his career as a singer.

For all the multiplicity of his talents and ambitions, however, and the evident maturation of his attitudes towards those who praise and pursue him, one further thread seems to run through all of Domingo's activities — a fundamental clue, perhaps, to what really makes him tick. One time in Madrid, I was watching him in rehearsal. For hour after hour he and his colleagues had to go through their music and moves as a new operatic production slowly took shape. By mid-evening, everyone (including me, and I was merely watching) began to flag, but not Domingo. He continued to act his part, make helpful suggestions, drop the occasional wisecrack in order to keep up everybody's spirits. I spotted his parents in the darkened auditorium and went over to chat with his mother. Where did Plácido get his tireless energy from? 'Oh, he was always like that,' said this tall, handsome woman with a smile, 'always performing, even as a child.'

We are all, to some extent, performers, and psychologists suggest that the desire in adulthood to perform, to display our talents in public, may be a primitive instinct, a residue of a childhood need, possibly even a sublimated form of sexual self-revelation. Certainly, many performing artists seem to be people who have managed to cultivate or retain into adulthood something of the innocent, open-minded responsiveness of childhood, the ability to combine youthful freshness of perception with the disciplined talent acquired with maturity.

Children's responses to people and things are not lessened by familiarity, and they create new words, new worlds, new categories to describe them. But children do not have the discipline or the organizational skills to create a satisfying whole out of these new perceptions. What children *can* do, however, is to perform, to show off skills, dress up, put on funny hats and voices, climb a tree, stick their tongues out, giggle and cry, and, in general, 'dramatize' — in effect, shout 'look at me!'.

All this activity adults dismiss as 'playing'. We tend to think of 'play' and 'games' as something children do because they are not capable, yet, of anything more serious. Adults only 'play' in their leisure time, an activity very much contrasted with the grown-up world of 'work'. However, playing games is a deep and essential part of human life, a voluntary activity (like art) that can help us impose some order upon a disordered world. We learn about military strategy by playing 'war games', learn about relationships with fellow beings by 'role playing' or by studying 'games people play', seek or confirm our national stereotypes from the way this or that country plays football, appreciate Brendel or Perlman playing Mozart or Beethoven. Is it just coincidence that all these seemingly unrelated activities are referred to as 'play', and is it going too far to suggest that they all have something in common with what children do in the nursery or playground? Is 'play' ultimately trivial?

Perhaps what these examples of 'playing' have in common is the fact that they all represent attempts to work one's way through a problem, by means of a series of more or less flexible rules, with the aim of being able to cope adequately with experiences presented to us by the outside world. We all 'play' with new experiences, knead them, mould them, bring earlier solutions temporarily to bear upon them and, by a dialectical process, come to impose order upon what was previously formless. This, in essence, is what a child does while 'playing', what we all do when faced with a new situation at work or at home, and, pre-eminently, what creative or interpret-ative artists do as they struggle to breathe life into, and mould new meaning out of, their fragmented material.

In addition, children typically have a richer fantasy life than do adults. Indeed, children sometimes cannot or will not differentiate fully between fantasy and reality. Here, too, the artist retains some-thing of the fantastical imagination of the child and weds it to the skills of discipline acquired with adulthood to create a new, imaginative synthesis of the two.

Thus, the artist is likely to have carried into adult life a valuable ability we all have in childhood but which most of us lose as we grow up, something of the freshness of response of a child, the inclination to use 'play' as a means of trying to impose order upon a stubbornly random world, and the capacity to create imaginative fantasy out of reality. The performing artist will, in addition, probably have in his or her make-up a vestige of the child's natural desire to call attention to itself, to show off, to appeal for adult approval by displaying its skills before others, whose role is to assess and, where appropriate, to allot praise, but not to participate.

These characteristics are not, of course, exclusive to 'artists', nor are they abnormal. We all share them to some extent and live richer lives in consequence. Childhood and adulthood, the worlds of fantasy and reality, of play and work, are interrelated, and the fulfilled and adjusted person will keep in touch with aspects of both throughout life. But whereas, if you were to repress the vestiges of childhood, you might still become a successful banker or oil execu-tive, you would be unlikely to permit your aesthetic instincts to express themselves fully and would be very unlikely to become a good performing artist. I am not, of course, saying that the per-forming artist is a childish or immature adult, although this is doubtless true of some, but rather that the performing artist is more likely to have retained some of the characteristics of childhood that many adults lose or undervalue.

In this, perhaps, lies an important key to the achievement, personal as well as aesthetic, of an interpretative artist like Domingo: that he is able to reconcile, to an unusual degree, the worlds of the child and the adult. Domingo, in performance as a singer, has the courage to let go of physical and emotional barriers, freeing enormous reserves of energy, but, at the same time, to control and direct this energy and never be at its mercy. This double-pronged ability helps explain why Domingo is such a great artist, but it is also an essential component of his off-stage personality. His capacity to give full weight to all aspects of his art, in other words, is merely the public manifestation of a remarkable inner balance between the exigencies of 'play' and 'work', expression and control, art and life. Ultimately, it is this temperamental equilibrium, not 'merely' the voice or the musicianship, that seems to form the foundation of Domingo's achievement. And it is this, perhaps, that has helped to give him the incentive, and the confidence, to add to his supreme mastery as a singer the additional subsidiary career as a conductor. He is, at core, a performer, a man on the move, who is obviously at his happiest and most fulfilled when, from stage or pit, he is at the heart of one of the great musico-dramatic showpieces to which he has devoted his life so generously; a gladiator riding atop two hundred horses. These are the moments above all, perhaps, when adult and child, man and artist, converge.

Usually in the run-up to a new production of an opera, music and production rehearsals tend to alternate. In some sessions, the singers will be coached, to piano accompaniment, by the conductor; in others, they will be blocking in the moves required for the staging. Gradually, the two sets of skills come together, the conductor and producer often attending each other's rehearsals. For a large, ambitious new production of a familiar work like *Bohème*, however, production rehearsals are probably bound to take precedence, especially, perhaps, when the conductor is also singing the tenor lead in another production being rehearsed simultaneously.

Domingo tells friends in Los Angeles that he has sung *Ballo* almost as often as *Bohème*, most recently on tour with the Metropolitan Opera in Japan a few months ago. He recalls learning the work in just three days back in 1967 when a colleague went sick and the Berlin Opera, with whom he was about to perform his début in *Aida*, asked if he could help them out by singing *Ballo* instead. Certainly, Plácido said, not wanting to admit that *Ballo* was not in his repertoire, and buried himself in the score. These Los Angeles performances are in a production borrowed from Covent Garden, which Domingo himself opened back in the mid-1970s.

The opera, written in 1857, revolves around the true story of the assassination of King Gustavus III of Sweden at a masked ball in 1792. The King is in love with Amelia, the wife of his most loyal minister, and she with him. Although, out of a sense of honour, their union is not consummated, the minister, on discovering their secret, joins the King's enemies and kills him. As the King dies, he nobly forgives his assailant and pronounces Amelia to have been innocent.

Political assassination was heady stuff in the late 1850s in an Italy shortly to throw off the yoke of Austrian rule, and Verdi and his librettist, Antonio Somma, were soon in trouble with the censors. The action had to be moved back in time and across the Atlantic, 'Gustavo' being demoted and becoming, instead, a mythical Governor of Colonial Boston called 'Riccardo'. The Covent Garden–Los Angeles production returns to the Sweden of Gustavus III, however, and pale blue and yellow predominate in the costumes and décor. Wherever and whenever the opera is placed, though, Verdi's powerful music summons up an atmosphere that is dark, northern, seafaring, with occasional glints of light flashing briefly between the lowering clouds. The King (or Governor) is popular, attractive, with a bright if somewhat volatile temperament — a wonderful role for Domingo. Gustavo and his court favourite, the page, Oscar (sung by a coloratura soprano), take all the courtiers off in disguise to visit a gypsy fortune-teller (one of Verdi's deep mezzos) whom some believe to be a witch. When she reads his palm and tells him he will shortly be killed by the first person to shake his hand, he laughs off her predictions. Two Acts later they come true.

No opera could be in stronger contrast to *La Bohème*: the urgent, assertive power of Verdi and the fragile vulnerability of Puccini; a King assassinated at a court ball by one of his ministers, and a little seamstress coughing herself to death with tuberculosis. In the Verdi opera, the precise location is of little significance; in *Bohème* it is of the essence. In Verdi there is a strong moral element — goodies and baddies, love and duty as Gustavo struggles with his conscience to do the right thing — whereas Puccini's characters are so innocent, so much more acted upon than acting. The Verdi score is full of high and noble sentiment; the Puccini packed with exquisite *fin de siècle* sentimentality.

Yet there are also similarities between the two works. Each contains a string of wonderful, memorable arias and set-piece ensembles interspersed with the most evocative and colourful scene painting. Dramatically, each pivots around a central, unfulfilled love story — 'I love you, but we must part', sings Gustavo to Amelia in *Ballo*, as does Mimì to Rodolfo in *Bohème*. In each, the composer has conjured up an imaginative and diverse orchestral palette, enabling him to create a rich and coherent musical world: Verdi's is noble, energetic, sombre, yet streaked with flashes of humour; Puccini's is quicksilver, impressionistic, poignant, vulnerable, but also full of humour used ironically to point up the tragedy.

Ballo has two casts and Domingo is in cast 'B'. This will enable him to conduct the opening night *Bohème* gala, have a day's rest when *Ballo* opens with cast 'A', sing *Ballo* the next night, and conduct the following day's *Bohème* matinée. Each opera has an open dress rehearsal or preview: *Bohème* an all-day affair before a house packed with children from Los Angeles schools, and *Ballo* (with the Domingo cast) the next evening in front of an audience specially made up from among LA's vast Hispanic community. These are important occasions to Domingo, who is conscious that many in these audiences will never have set foot in this magnificent theatre or been to opera before. At the *Bohème* run-through, he receives a huge round of applause from the schoolchildren, most of whom are from Los Angeles' ethnic minorities. I sat among them in the upper reaches of the house and they seemed to be enjoying themselves hugely. I don't know what they made of the opera, though they laughed at all the jokes, were impeccably silent during Mimì's death scene, and gave everyone a big ovation at the end. Maestro Domingo, of course, received a massive roar from the excited children, and I can report with confidence that they adored having the opportunity to spend a few hours of their lives inside the pure luxury of the Dorothy Chandler Pavilion.

It is Thursday evening, 9 September 1993. A red carpet stretches across the plaza outside the Music Center to bear the rich and/or famous of Los Angeles as they walk from their cars to the Dorothy Chandler Pavilion where the curtain will shortly go up for the gala opening night of the season, the new LAMCO production of *La Bohème*. Helicopters circle overhead, though whether or not the airborne police or newsmen are more interested in the illuminati arriving at the opera or the angry crowd picketing the Department of Water and Power opposite is a moot point, much discussed at ground level.

The Chandler Pavilion represents a self-conscious attempt to marry the grandiloquence of modern America with the elegance and opulence of nineteenth-century Europe. For a venue with over 3200 seats, the auditorium retains a surprising degree of intimacy. A massive, movable acoustic canopy extends outwards from the top of the proscenium arch to control and direct the flow of sound, while the towering side walls of butternut wood also help give the audience a sense of being enveloped in music. Wherever you sit in the house, the sounds and pictures from the stage reach you with remarkable clarity (unless you have tickets towards the sides of the back ten rows in the orchestra stalls, in which case part of the stage and supertitles above the arch will be hidden from view by the overhanging Founders' Circle above).

The grandeur of the auditorium is, if anything, surpassed by that of the foyers, with busts of Stravinsky, Heifetz, Klemperer and many others, the gold and white mosaic tiled columns and marble façades gratefully embedded with the gold-embossed names of 'Founders'. As you stroll through the centre of the grand foyer, your footsteps and conversation will reverberate beneath a golden acoustic dome that helps create the illusion that even a small crowd constitutes an excited throng—an impression reinforced by the many mirrors that reflect, in an infinite number of images and from all directions, your progress up the grand stairway. On the stairs and in the Grand Hall above the first level, an olive-green pile carpet may absorb noise. But everywhere else is an orgy of bright, shiny surfaces, especially glass—not just the mirrors, but plate glass along the banisters and balustrades and in the vast floor-to-ceiling east-facing wall; glistening crystal in the three massive chandeliers; and a plethora of diamond-shaped glass cut-outs liberally placed at reflective angles on the multi-curved ceiling above. Just to complete the subtle sense of discreet activity on a bed of placid opulence, the continuous sound of a fountain in the entrance hall washes through the entire edifice, as though to parallel or echo the dancing columns of water that envelop the giant Jacques Lipschitz sculpture representing Peace on Earth in the sun-drenched plaza outside.

Backstage, there is a buzz of excitement as the minutes tick away. Ross glides round the dressing rooms, wishing everyone good luck. Sirianni is there early, his hair in a net as the make-up department make him look even younger and slimmer. Esperian is early, too, practising *arpeggios* and looking and sounding far more fresh and vibrant than any woman has a right to do a mere ten weeks after giving birth. Plácido Domingo turns up, clutching what looks like the entire contents of a flower shop, and beams warmly at welcoming friends. Downstairs, violinists and cellists sip coffee from a drinks machine or share tostado chips with grubby-faced Parisian street urchins and their bewigged 'mothers'. 'The freeway was terrible today,' complains one of the mothers, desperate for another coffee, as her stage son slips off into the dressing room reserved for 'Super Boys, Super Men, Musician Men & Chorus Boys'. A 'weightlifter' munches a sandwich and glances at the sports results.

The tannoy calls Act I beginners to the stage while warning bells ring in the front of house. A few minutes later, the auditorium lights dim, and Plácido Domingo walks down through the chorus cafeteria and thence up the dark stairway towards the orchestra pit. 'Are you ready, Maestro?', asks the stage manager courteously. 'We'd better be!' Domingo quips, checking his white tie, and then strides out to the conductor's rostrum, acknowledges the applause and shakes the hand of his Concert Master. He raises his baton, cello bows quiver expectantly, and then, with a single down beat, we're off once more into the enchanting bitter-sweet world of Puccini's immortal young lovers. Sirianni and Black, as Rodolfo and Marcello, get the opera off to a vigorous start, joined soon by fellow bohemians John Atkins and Richard Bernstein, as Schaunard and Colline. Esperian arrives and quickly establishes herself as a singing actress of the top rank. Her *pianissimo* high note at the very end of Act I is itself worth the price of a ticket, though few in the auditorium hear it as it is drowned by premature applause.

The scene change to the Café Momus scene lasts a cool four minutes, and then Domingo brings in the brash trumpet chords that inaugurate the hardest of the four Acts to carry off successfully. The opening chorus of street-sellers looks good (leaving no space unfilled!) and the vocal ensemble is impeccable. Tatyana Odinokova's arrival in her jalopy causes a minor sensation and Odinokova herself a major one. Eyebrows are raised at one or two of Ross' more controversial pieces of business, but the sheer panache of the zouave band and the plethora of French flags provide an invigorating coda.

Domingo is beaming during the interval, happy with his singers, chorus and orchestra. He can't wait for the opera to continue. The curtain rises on a snowy Act III to music that is now cold, bleak, empty. Esperian has become a truly pathetic figure as she overhears Sirianni telling Black how her cough will kill her, and then sings him her heart-breaking 'Farewell' aria, while the horseplay in the last Act, the shock of Mimì's sudden arrival, Colline's simple song of farewell to his coat (beautifully judged by Bernstein) and the death of Mimì all work their magic.

The maestro is pleased. Backstage, afterwards, he is besieged with congratulations from friends and wellwishers. Ross comes round (accompanied by his wife, Lee Radziwill, sister of Jackie Kennedy) and the two men embrace, each smiling broadly. 'I'll be along soon!', Domingo promises as Ross and his wife make their way out to the post-performance party that has been arranged out on the plaza, though it is, in fact, another hour before he, Marta, and their friends and family are finally able to leave the dressing room.

Outside, the plaza has been transformed into a nineteenth-century Parisian street replete with can-can dancers, jugglers, an orchestra in red bandbox uniforms, *fin de siècle* street lamps and more than enough bistro-style pâté, crudités, boeuf bourguignon and crème brulée to feed *le tout Montmartre*—or at least such luminaries as Candice Bergen, Angelica Huston, Efrem Zimbalist Junior, Kathy Bates, Sam Wanamaker, David Hockney, Kirk Douglas, Henry Mancini, Jack Valenti, and about 600 other wealthy and/or beautiful operaphiles. And who (people ask) is that dashing young man with the chic wife, both in sleek black? Don't I know that face? Shortly, a party-stopping rendition of 'Happy Birthday' to one of the revellers reveals this to be Sirianni, miraculously transformed from emaciation to elegance. In another part of 'Paris-on-the-plaza', Esperian, even more miraculously transformed from death to life, meets film star Kathy Bates, while Odinokova cuts as impressive a swathe wherever she turns in this version of Paris as she had in the other one earlier on.

As the vivacious *bonhomie bohèmienne* finally comes to an end, Hemmings reflects that his maestro, director, cast, and company have given the Los Angeles Opera a spectacular and memorable opening night. Theirs is a vibrant, young company, eager for the success that is now coming its way. In another four years, if things go according to schedule, a new auditorium—the Disney Hall—will be opened across from the Dorothy Chandler Pavilion to house the LA Philharmonic. Every morning, Hemmings looks gleefully out from his office to watch as the building work progresses. When the Philharmonic finally moves out of the Chandler and into Disney Hall, the opera company will become the Pavilion's one principal tenant and will then be free to expand to more than a hundred performances a season.

As Hemmings bids goodnight to Domingo, he considers the huge impact his Artistic Consultant has already had on the LA Opera and how important Domingo's presence is to the future of the company. The two men shake hands warmly. 'Look after yourself, Plácido,' says Hemmings, knowing that Domingo has had a bit of a cold. After all, tonight's conductor must be back in a couple of days to sing the lead in *Ballo*. Domingo smiles reassuringly, buoyed up by the palpable success of tonight's *Bohème*. He feels fine, he says.

At last, Domingo goes back with Marta to their nearby apartment for some rest, yet already his mind is beginning to concentrate on his next engagement. In a couple of weeks' time, he has another opening, another show, this time in New York. The 1993 Metropolitan Opera Gala, to be broadcast around the world, will celebrate the twenty-fifth anniversary of débuts there by both Domingo and Pavarotti, and each tenor has undertaken to deliver something special. Then, after the Gala, Domingo has another Met assignment that is, in its own way, just as demanding: a new production of Verdi's *Stiffelio*, an opera unknown to New York audiences and, until recently, to himself. Above all, the following spring, a very special Met occasion beckons—the unveiling at that greatest of opera houses of a new production of what many consider the finest opera ever written, one that also contains Domingo's noblest role: Verdi's *Otello*.

3

The Moor at the Met

'ESULTATE!'

This is the clarion call of triumph with which Otello, early in the Verdi masterwork that bears his name, trumpets his first appearance. 'Exult', cries the General, flushed with victory, as he steps on to land following a fearsome storm at sea, for we have successfully defeated the proud fleet of the infidel, and off he goes again, amidst choral cries of 'Vittoria!'.

The opening few minutes of *Otello* are perhaps the most powerful in all opera. The chorus, watching the elemental battle from the shore, pours out its fears, hopes and prayers in a crashing maelstrom of musical inventiveness. Then, in a contrast of ineffable nobility, comes the tenor's magniloquent solo cry, 'Esultate!'.

The first time this glorious phrase rang out from the stage of the Metropolitan Opera, New York, during the 1993–4 season, was at the Gala opening night, 27 September 1993, and it came from the lips not of Plácido Domingo, universally acknowledged as the greatest Otello in recent times, but of a man who had never sung the role on stage before: Luciano Pavarotti. Every year, at the start of the season, the Met holds a fundraising evening at which its current idols perform for a wealthy and adoring public. This particular year, however, this public had eyes and ears for two stars in particular, both celebrating the twenty-fifth anniversary of their Met débuts: Pavarotti and Domingo.

Domingo was the first of the two men to appear at the Met and he remembers the occasion well. It was September 1968, and the young tenor and his family were living in Teaneck, New Jersey, just across the Hudson River. In those days Domingo was on the roster of the New York City Opera, the Met's sister house across the plaza at Lincoln Center, where, that week, he was singing *Il Tabarro* and *I Pagliacci*, as well as covering performances for the Met. He recalls arriving home one Saturday afternoon after a long stage rehearsal for *Turandot*. The phone went and Domingo heard the voice of Rudolf Bing, General Manager of the Metropolitan. To this day, he remembers the conversation more or less word for word:

'Plácido,' said Bing in his quiet, authoritative Austrian tones, 'how are you feeling?'

'I'm fine, Mr Bing, thank you.'

'Good. Because you have to go on tonight.' (This was just four days before Domingo was officially scheduled to make his Met début as Maurizio in Cilèa's opera *Adriana Lecouvreur*.)

'No, Mr Bing, it's not tonight,' said Domingo, and, when Bing persisted, 'But I can't, Mr Bing. I haven't warmed up today, and besides . . .'

'Plácido, you have to. Franco's just called to say he's sick and can't sing Maurizio tonight.' (Franco Corelli, a wonderful tenor in the heroic mould, suffered badly from nerves and had a reputation for cancelling.)

'Please come at once,' Bing added, with just the right combination of insistence and courtesy.

Domingo recalls that he was angry and did not believe that Corelli was really ill. Furthermore, as the *Turandot* rehearsal had been for the staging, he had not sung all day and his voice had not had a chance to limber up. Those arriving early at the Met were already ambling towards their seats. They had been told that Corelli was being replaced by the young Domingo and were asked to be patient as Domingo was at that very moment driving back into town and would be ready very soon.

On the way, while he was driving, Domingo sang a few scales and *arpeggios* to warm up his voice. He tells amusing stories of the reactions of fellow drivers who stopped alongside him at traffic lights. One was on his way to the Met and worried that he would be late: 'It's O K,' laughed Plácido, as the light turned green, 'they won't start until I get there!', and he sped off down the avenue.

During the next quarter century, Domingo was to appear at the Metropolitan every season in a total of 367 performances of 34 different roles. In the early years, his Met repertoire included not only *Adriana*, but also *Il Trovatore*, *Turandot*, *Cavalleria Rusticana*, *I Pagliacci*, *Andrea Chénier*, *Don Carlo*, *Les Contes d'Hoffmann*, *I Vespri Siciliani*, *La Bohème*, *Lucia*, *La Traviata*, *Ernani*, *Faust*, *Luisa Miller*, *Roméo et Juliette*, *Rigoletto*, *Werther* and *Manon Lescaut*. His first Met appearances in *Tosca* date back to 1969, *Ballo* to 1970, *Aida* and *Carmen* to 1971. Eventually, in 1979, came Domingo's first Met *Otello*.

Pavarotti's Met début (in *La Bohème*) was a couple of months after Domingo's and he, too, soon became a regular and immensely popular guest. By the early 1970s, both men were firm favourites with Metropolitan audiences and, before long, were being described by the press as operatic rivals. Neither man would talk publicly about the other in these terms; indeed, for years, each studiously avoided mentioning the other in interviews. 'There's plenty of room in the world for two, three, five, ten or twenty good tenors,' they would each say to inquisitive interviewers, and then change the subject. The fact remains, however, that the two of them were set up as a sort of prize fight, especially, perhaps, in New York, and the result was the greatest operatic spectator sport since Callas and Tebaldi were rallying their respective troops in Milan and Rome a quarter of a century previously.

Domingo and Pavarotti have careers that contain curious par-allels, curious because, on the face of it, it would seem that the differences are far greater. Pavarotti is Italian, Domingo Spanish but raised in Mexico. Pavarotti is more than five years older than Domingo, which is a long time in the life of a singer. Pavarotti's early experiences of opera were in provincial Italy, then he graduated through places like Glyndebourne, Dublin and Australia to Covent Garden, while Domingo started out in Mexico, Israel, and then, via Hamburg and elsewhere in middle Europe, gained his first real recognition in the USA. Vocally, Pavarotti has a higher, lyric tenor ideally suited to the operas of Bellini, Donizetti and early Verdi, and indeed, except for *Bohème* and *Tosca*, he has infrequently ventured outside this domain. Domingo's natural musical habitat starts where Pavarotti's tends to tail off, in mid nineteenth-century Italian opera, and includes a vast amount besides this, including major works from the French and German repertoires. Pavarotti's entire recording career has been virtually exclusively managed by Decca, while Domingo tried exclusivity to R C A for a few years but soon abandoned it, preferring a series of *ad hoc* contracts with whichever company seemed to offer the most attractive terms at the time.

On stage, Pavarotti, always recognizably himself, has sung some thirty-odd major roles; Domingo, who has a deserved reputation as an accomplished and dedicated actor, has performed over eighty. Pavarotti's most famous part, certainly the one that helped shoot him to fame at Covent Garden and later the Metropolitan, was that of Tonio in Donizetti's light and frothy *La Fille du Régiment*, with its string of nine successive top Cs, while, in later years, he tended to concentrate on roles like Nemorino, the lovelorn peasant boy in the same composer's *L'Elisir d'Amore*. Domingo, for all his immense versatility, has always been more associated with darker, more tragic operatic roles — Canio in *Pagliacci*, Don José in *Carmen*, and, above all, Otello.

Now, though, consider the parallels. The two men not only made their New York Metropolitan Opera débuts just a few weeks apart, but were soon finding their way on to the same television chat shows, each opening the Met or Scala season or recording albums of popular songs. Pavarotti sang with Frank Sinatra, Domingo with John Denver. In 1980, Pavarotti starred in the Met's biggest show, its free *Rigoletto* in Central Park; a year later, the opening of the Met's 'Opera in the Park' featured Domingo in *Tosca*.

There are personal parallels, too. Domingo has three sons; Pavarotti three daughters. Domingo's parents were *zarzuela* performers, his mother particularly well-known. Pavarotti's father was a talented amateur tenor who might have made a professional career if circumstances had been different. 'Domingo sings to please his mother, Pavarotti his father', said a colleague of both, whose wit perhaps exceeded her sagacity. Each man has said that the label 'world's greatest tenor' that the press, particularly in America, insists on sticking on them is unimportant and irrelevant, and each has pronounced, safely and predictably enough, that the world's greatest tenor was, in any case, Enrico Caruso. By 1980, each had become a multi million-dollar international business and a household name throughout the musical world.

If only opera were immune from the overblown partisanships that feature in the world of spectator sports — but, of course, it is not. Pavarotti and Domingo are simply victims — as well as beneficiaries — of a pattern that recurs throughout history. At the time of Handel, back in the 1720s, the main topic of musical gossip concerned the respective merits (and egos and fees) of the two great rival *prime donne*, Faustina and Cuzzoni. Two hundred years later, Gigli was to recount how 'with grim amusement' he read two advertisements that appeared in the New York press on the same day a few years after the death of Caruso. One said, 'Gigli, the world's greatest tenor, will sing at a benefit recital for the Italian Hospital on Sunday afternoon, February 16th'. The other said, 'Martinelli, the world's greatest tenor, will sing at a benefit recital for the Relief Society for the Aged at the Waldorf Astoria Hotel on February 26th'. Gigli's was one of the most effortlessly mellifluous voices the world had ever heard, Martinelli's one of the noblest, and people between the wars could also have had the pleasure of hearing (among others) Pertile, Cortis, Fleta, Crimi, Tauber, Melchior and Schipa. However, as Gigli added ruefully, 'Impresarios have a fondness for publicity-catching labels'.

Things have not changed — they still do. Whoever invented the title of Pavarotti's solo album 'King of the High Cs' deserves a medal of a sort. Certainly, Pavarotti's outstanding ability with the high notes won him his early popular fame, but the 'King of the High Cs' implied more. There was the buccaneering image, the suggestion of swagger and swag, that played its part in endearing Pavarotti to a general public who had not come across him before. Above all, of course, there was the suggestion that he was the best, the King. It was to be some years before *Newsweek* magazine would finally dub Domingo on its cover the 'King of the Opera'.

Once Pavarotti had conquered the American public, he made the New York Metropolitan his base. He sang elsewhere, of course, but the Met was 'home'. He also hired an astute, some would say ruthless, New York-based manager, Herbert Breslin. Breslin was the experienced manager of some of the biggest stars, and Pavarotti willingly put himself into his hands. The results were soon apparent as a public image became established and American audiences got used to seeing Pavarotti's burly shape emerging on to the concert platform, arms raised in the style of a prize fighter or the victorious General de Gaulle, large white handkerchief—'my security blanket', Pavarotti called it—held aflutter.

Within a few years, Pavarotti was also appearing on all the big television shows in the USA, and on the cover of the big-circulation weeklies, riding a horse as Grand Marshal at the head of New York's Columbus Day Parade, advertising American Express cards on television or Blackglama Furs, singing at the Academy Awards ceremony, pictured in the glossies sweeping up the snow in the winter or playing tennis with John McEnroe in the summer.

Domingo's career took a different direction. He did less than Pavarotti in that he never gave frequent concerts, but the amount of operatic work Domingo undertook from the outset surpassed virtually everyone else's efforts. His repertoire was soon larger than that of any other major tenor except, perhaps, Nicolai Gedda, and Domingo strove to sing at most of his favourite places every year, as if anxious to enable his admirers to see him sooner or later in all his major roles, wherever opera was produced.

Domingo, like Pavarotti, learned the publicity value of appearing on television chat shows, allowing his name and face to be used to advertise various products, doing what the publicity people call 'PAs'—public appearances—signing records and photos, and starring in television variety specials. Pavarotti and Domingo may both have protested that they disliked the alleged rivalry that had been set up between them, but it strained credulity to be told that neither of them deliberately contributed to it. Several times—for example, the very week that Domingo was to open in an important new production—some glossy publication in the same city would just happen to run a major feature on Pavarotti. 'You can't tell me that that was coincidence,' Domingo would mutter, and add, with an attempt at a smile, 'Mind you, I suppose it's flattering in a way that they feel they need to do this to me.'

On one occasion, the programmes for one of Domingo's performances contained a large advertisement for Pavarotti's record company provocatively announcing their man to be 'the world's greatest tenor'. Domingo, normally restrained in his reactions, insisted that the offending advertisement be removed from the programmes or he would not sing. Needless to say, it was removed.

Domingo, a natural conciliator, was at first ill-inclined to enter the ring and fight back. 'If the public want to compare us,' he would say, confident of his supreme all-round artistry, 'they can come to our performances and judge for themselves.' Yet, bit by bit, he appeared to enter the hustings. It was not a decision reached in a single blinding moment of rage or truth. Rather, it was the result of a combination of seemingly unrelated decisions made in and around the early 1980s. As the Barcelona Liceo went through a rocky time, for example, and Domingo found himself turning down opportunities of singing there while being offered attractive pro-ductions at the Metropolitan, he and Marta decided to make their main family home in New York. At about the same time, record producer Milton Okun persuaded Domingo to consider recording an album of popular American songs. Meanwhile, Domingo had recently switched publicity agents in both London and New York, and, especially in the latter, was soon the recipient of a growing amount of media attention.

The Domingo counter-attack, if that was what it was, was swift, powerful, effective, and at first, perhaps, overdone. Domingo was later to feel that he may have overreacted when, for example, Kurt Herbert Adler, boss of the San Francisco Opera, said in public that he thought Pavarotti the greatest tenor in the world and Domingo, for a time, refused to sing there. The incident with the Pavarotti advertisements in the Domingo programmes, similarly, produced anger in Domingo that was understandable at the time but which he later felt it might have been wiser to defuse. However, the more positive aspects—the visible presence in New York, a growing number of performances at the Metropolitan Opera, the pop recordings, the TV appearances and Rolex watch adver-tisements—mostly did Domingo a power of good, and led to a self-perpetuating snowball of favourable publicity. Events, moreover, seemed to play into his hands as Pavarotti had a poor reception for some performances during this period, cancelled others, and made a much-heralded, but little praised, commercial movie called *Yes Giorgio!*

Both men were frequently featured in the glossy magazines and on television, with varying degrees of success. For example, Pavarotti did an embarrassing TV show in which sundry famous friends passed through his happy home in Modena; Domingo took on a live TV homage to Caruso in which he was clearly nervous and below his best. The list of what were essentially publicity appearances by Domingo became much longer, and not only in the USA. He managed to fly to Paris, for example, at considerable personal inconvenience, on the morning of President Mitterrand's inauguration, quickly learn the words of the 'Marseillaise', and, later in the day, sing the anthem splendidly ('with all the fire of a committed Socialist!', said one incredulous bystander) to tens of thousands of spectators and, of course, countless millions of television viewers. It is hard to resist opportunities like this when they come your way—the chance of being fêted by President Mitterrand, the Pope or the Queen Mother, or watched by millions as you hand out the Oscars on worldwide TV, play football with Maximilian Schell, Kevin Keegan or Hans Krankl, or exchange wisecracks and songs with Carol Burnett or Miss Piggy. *All* publicity, the saying goes, is *good* publicity, and Domingo succeeded in becoming a major celebrity, whose name, face and voice were familiar to millions in every corner of the developed world.

Not quite as familiar as those of Luciano Pavarotti, however, with his reassuringly bulky figure, broad, toothy grin, and fluttering white handkerchief. Pavarotti, sticking carefully to a small repertoire of Italian songs and operas that suit his lyrical voice and sunny personality, had a kind of mass-market appeal that the darker, deeper, more questing artistic style of Domingo could not quite achieve, however many chat shows and Hollywood spectaculars he appeared on. Domingo continued to widen his operatic repertoire, recorded more pop records, turned to German song, did more conducting, and took on several opera films. Pavarotti, by contrast, guided by a single manager and a single record company, focused on the few things he did best.

Of course, operagoers had long been aware that there were not just two good tenors before the public, but several. It depended what you were looking for. As dramatic tenors like Vickers or high, lyrical tenors like Kraus or Gedda were approaching the ends of their careers, and Domingo and Pavarotti reaching the crown of theirs, younger men were also beginning to climb the ladder. One whose feet were already especially secure there was José Carreras, a man whose combination of youthful ardour and poignant lyricism in operas like *La Bohème*, *La Traviata* or *Un Ballo in Maschera* were outstanding. There was something plaintive in his singing, a suggestion of a tear in the voice at moments of high passion that more than compensated for the occasional scoop or wobble he allowed himself. There was something plaintive, too, in the slim figure of a man who must clearly have resented being excluded from speculation about the 'world's greatest tenor'. Everywhere Carreras appeared on stage, he was greeted with rapture, yet it was never *he* who was first choice to star in this TV show or that recording: 'We're only third in world tenors,' he sometimes seemed to be saying, with some bitterness, 'so we try harder'.

Like Domingo, Carreras is a Spaniard. Unlike Domingo, he is a Catalan, a protegé of Montserrat Caballé and her influential agent brother, Carlos. 'My adopted son', Caballé used to call him as they sang operas like *Tosca* together. Another person who helped mould Carreras' career was Herbert von Karajan, who invited him to the Salzburg Festival to sing more muscular works like *Carmen*, *Don Carlos* and *Aida*. As time passed, Carreras began to build up an impressive discography (for Philips) and strove to achieve the wider public recognition that was clearly his due. Then, in 1987, he fell ill with leukemia.

For a long time it seemed Carreras would die. Literally hundreds of thousands of admirers from all over the world wrote to him with great affection, encouraging him in his struggle for life. Both Pavarotti and Domingo visited Carreras, spoke to him on the phone whenever they could, and offered him hope, practical help and genuine goodwill. When news began to filter out that, against the odds, Carreras had a slim chance of winning his desperate fight for survival, there was worldwide admiration for his courage. Then, one evening, during the interval of a performance of *Fedora* with Domingo at the Liceo in Barcelona in March 1988, Domingo came out, hushed the packed audience and told them there was a very special friend in the house who wished to come on stage and say hello. He went over to the wings and, in a scene of immense emotional intensity, returned, embracing a desperately frail and emaciated, but ecstatically happy, José Carreras.

The illness of Carreras and his almost miraculous recovery proved a turning point, not only in his own life, but also in those of Domingo and Pavarotti. They had all felt brushed by death, faced by the stark fact of their own mortality. Whatever resentments may have divided the three men in earlier years were transcended by the deeper humanity, tempered by misfortune, that now united them. For Domingo, Carreras' ordeal had occurred only a couple of years after the Mexican earthquake in which members of his own family had died, and not long after the death of his father. It was a sobering period, and clearly a time for solidarity rather than rivalry. When, even more miraculously it seemed, Carreras actually resumed his career as a singer in 1989, both Pavarotti and Domingo sincerely wished him well. I remember visiting Vienna in January 1990, when Carreras was appearing at the State Opera (in *Carmen*) for the first time since his illness, and Domingo was singing *Lohengrin*. The two men appeared together at a gala, the high point of which was a duet from *Cavalleria Rusticana*, sung by Carreras and Agnes Baltsa, which Domingo conducted. The evening ended with a host of stars on stage singing the 'Brindisi' from *La Traviata*, with Domingo and Carreras laughingly alternating the tenor line. A month later, I was at the New York Metropolitan Opera where, one memorable Saturday, Pavarotti sang the Duke in *Rigoletto* at the broadcast matinée, sharing the Principal Tenor's dressing room that day with Domingo, who took up occupation for that evening's performance of *Samson et Dalila*. While in New York, Domingo was also rehearsing *Otello*. There, in the darkened auditorium, was Pavarotti. Pavarotti was shortly to try out this most demanding of tenor parts himself, not on stage, but in concert performances, under Solti in Chicago and New York, and he was keen to learn as much as he could from the acknowledged master of the title role.

That summer, all three tenors appeared on the same bill in a massively publicized concert at the Caracalla Baths in Rome under the baton of Zubin Mehta, televised live all over the world on the eve of the World Cup soccer final. The three men took it in turns to sing arias and songs, touching hands soccer-style as one would come off stage and the next go on. All three were in superb form, and there was a warmth and generosity of spirit between them that would have been unthinkable before Carreras' illness. The evening ended with a medley of popular songs and arias with parts for all three tenors. The subsequent CD, cassette and video of this extraordinary event not only broke all records for sales of classical music, but, unlike any previous operatic recordings, climbed to the top of the popular music charts as well. Nothing remotely like this had ever happened before. Opera was, henceforth, mass entertainment, big business, and the three tenors concerned were guaranteed world superstar status wherever they went. It was clearly better to be overt friends and colleagues than covert rivals.

Pavarotti went on to do his *Otello* concerts in Chicago and New York, and, despite being ill at the first of them, acquitted himself well, not only singing the love duet in Act I with melting lyricism, but also finding a dramatic intensity for the later Acts that surprised and impressed the sceptics. At the Met Gala in 1991, he and Domingo came together, at the end of a wonderful evening, to sing the male voice duet from Act IV of *La Bohème*. A couple of years later, when the Met Gala focused on the twenty-fifth anniversary of the début of both men, Domingo sang Act I of *Die Walküre* for the first time in America, with Meier as his Sieglinde, while Pavarotti, singing Act I of *Otello* on stage for the first time anywhere, was partnered by Esperian as Desdemona. The evening culminated with what must rank as one of the strangest performances ever given of Act III of *Il Trovatore* — the two tenors alternating as Manrico and singing in unison the famous top C at the end of 'Di quella pira!'. The audience loved it, as did the press and the millions around the world who were to hear this memorable evening on radio, and so, obviously, did the two central figures of attention, Plácido Domingo and Luciano Pavarotti.

It was courageous of Pavarotti to sing *Otello*, especially on a bill shared with Domingo, and the gesture was widely appreciated. It was not, however, an opera that he was ever likely to absorb into his repertoire, and when, later in the 1993–4 season, the Metropolitan unveiled its new production of Verdi's penultimate opera, it was, inevitably, with Domingo in the leading role.

Nine-thirty in the morning. The almost empty Metropolitan Opera auditorium is alive with the reverberating sound of vacuum cleaners as a small army of women work their way through the detritus of the previous evening. On stage, a posse of strong men — pushing, pulling, shouting to distant colleagues, and brandishing a whole armoury of screwdrivers, scissors, knives, hacksaws and hammers — gradually transform last night's Seville into this morning's Cyprus.

If you walk back across the side stage, weaving your way gingerly between towering Bohemian chimneys and Spanish haciendas, you will encounter taverna tables laden with platters bearing mountains of hummus, authentic down to the bed of vine leaves and topped with olives — all so realistic that, up close, one is tempted to sneak a fingerful. On another table, yellowing parchment documents, regally inscribed, lie in waiting for this morning's rehearsal alongside late medieval wall maps, a quill pen or two, a telescope and a model sailing ship. Sets and props at the Met are far more complicated and realistic nowadays than they were thirty years ago. In the old Met, many shows were dressed with, essentially, painted flats (flat sections of scenery mounted on a frame) that could comfortably be trucked off to a warehouse in New Jersey until the next time they were needed. Today, as many of the Met's productions are shot for television and video, sets have to be more realistically textured, and every document or door handle, every crucifix, cannon ball or cuff-link (let alone a plate of hummus) has to look the part.

From the very back of the stage, through the little doorway that leads to the artists' dressing rooms, Domingo appears. He is wearing blue jeans, a blue sweater and shirt, and a pair of comfortable brown loafers. He takes a look at some of the *Otello* props, a winged lion here, a gun emplacement there, the hummus and maps, has a word with a passing electrician, who warns him not to trip over a pair of running wires, and saunters forwards towards the side door in the wings, stage left, that leads into the auditorium.

Many years ago, Laurence Olivier said of Domingo, in amazed admiration, that he 'acts the role of Othello as well as I do — and can sing it as well!' Domingo's awesome reputation, above all in this role, is a heavy burden to bear. He slips into the darkened Met auditorium, settles into a seat in the fifth row, and watches quietly as the conductor signals to a pianist to begin.

The Met chorus, initially all male and indistinguishable from the stage hands except that there are more of them, pour out their passions, and are soon joined by the women. Domingo keeps his counsel, watches the scene, absorbs the atmosphere, then walks back through the doorway that links auditorium to stage just in time to come on, completely in character, to deliver a full-voiced 'Esultate!'. The greatest operatic ship ever designed is being launched once more, and this time its home berth is to be the New York Metropolitan Opera.

Many, and not just Americans, consider the New York Metropolitan to be the world's premier opera house. How, though, can such a claim be assessed? Well, the Met is certainly one of the biggest. The present house, opened in 1966, has an overall audience capacity of over 4000 people, who face a proscenium stage picture 54 feet (16.4 m) square at the back and on either side of which are three more full-size stages where sets can be pre-assembled, ready for fast scene changes. In a typical season, the Met gives some 208 performances of 23–25 different operas over a 30-week period, another 15 or 20 on tour abroad to Germany or Japan (though no longer around America), plus a further handful given free in the parks of New York and New Jersey during the summer. Throughout the season, there is opera every night except Sunday, and there is always a Saturday matinée, broadcast for over half a century throughout the USA and, latterly, to much of Europe as well. Running the Met costs close to $130 million a year. Of this, two-thirds can normally be recouped from box office receipts, much of the rest from private contributions — small, large, and very large — and a tiny fraction from federal, state and city government agencies. In a good year, the system will just about break even. A few years ago, the Met management set up a $100 million endowment fund as a hedge against inflation and/or recession, virtually every penny of which comes from private sources. None of the world's other leading opera houses operates without substantial government funding, certainly in Europe. Indeed, Covent Garden, La Scala, Vienna, Paris or Munich would cease to function if they had to rely on private contributions for so large a part of their income.

The Met was not the first in its field in New York. Indeed, it has its origins in the reaction of New York's *nouveau riche* against the reigning opera house of the 1850s–1870s, the Academy of Music on Irving Place and 14th Street (where the Con Edison building now stands). All the great operas and singers could be heard at the Academy of Music, but not all of New York's high society could be seen there for the Academy had only a small number of boxes, and those who wanted to put the finishing touches to their status within that society *had* to have — that is, own, more or less in perpetuity — a box at the opera. With the influx of new industrial wealth into the thriving city during the post-Civil War 'Gilded Age', a number of the rich, famous and deprived decided to build a new, larger opera house, *their* opera house, a wonderful palace where the finest opera could be heard and the most expensive furs and tiaras seen. As society moved uptown, so did the opera. The new house was accordingly built on 39th Street and Broadway, and if its yellow brick exterior looked like an office block or factory, its opulent interior featured the all-important horseshoes containing a total of over a hundred boxes. The New York Metropolitan Opera opened on 22 October 1883 (a few months after the opening of the Brooklyn Bridge) with a season of Italian opera. The gala opening night featured a popular French work, Gounod's *Faust*, performed in Italian.

The Met's opening season was an artistic triumph and a financial disaster. The boxholders paid a fortune for their privileges, of course, but the top singers of the Italian repertoire commanded very high fees and the Met's 3000-odd *non*-box seats invariably could not find buyers. So, the Manager was fired and a new regime installed by the stockholders, which proceeded for several seasons to give everything — including the Italian and French repertoire — in German. German singers came more cheaply than Italian ones, and there were, in any case, wonderful new German works, notably most of late Wagner, lining up to be performed in the USA for the first time. New York at the time was still largely a white, Anglo-

Saxon city, populated by people of North European extraction, and it seemed that more seats would be sold at the opera if works were offered in German than in Italian. Wagner had died the year the Met opened, and, throughout the 1890s, the American musical establishment made the annual pilgrimage to the Bayreuth Festspielhaus to soak up the legacy of the Master. For many years, though, the most popular of all operas presented at the Met continued to be *Faust*. Yet this, too, now had to be performed in German, and the wits of New York dubbed the Met their 'Faustspielhaus'.

Several times, the Met nearly closed. The building was said to be fireproof, but much of its interior went up in a huge blaze in 1892. The trouble was that the building itself *was* fireproof, so there was nothing the stockholders could really do except undertake a costly interior renovation in time for the 1893–4 season. Between 1906 and 1909, years when Enrico Caruso reigned at the Met, the impresario Oscar Hammerstein (uncle of Richard Rodgers' famous lyricist) built a rival opera house down the road and lured some of the best-known singers of the day. The Met survived, partly because Caruso remained loyal and partly because the Met decided to buy Hammerstein out for a large sum. A quarter of a century later, the gods made another attempt to close the Met, this time assuming the form not of fire or rivalry, but of Depression. In desperation, General Manager Gatti-Casazza requested that everyone work for markedly less pay. Everyone did (except Gigli, who left the company).

Through all this — and through the two World Wars, during which German and other singers were unavailable and/or unwelcome in the USA — the Met survived. In San Francisco, on its 1906 spring tour, the Met company, including Caruso, had finished a performance of *Carmen* one evening when earthquake and fire devastated the city and the very theatre in which they had just been performing. Nobody in the company was hurt and the Met paid all its artists off in full, bringing them safely back to New York. Caruso vowed never to sing in San Francisco again. I wonder what he would have thought if he had been present at the Met on the night of 4 March 1960.

The opera was Verdi's *La Forza del Destino*, starring the American singers Leonard Warren and Richard Tucker with Renata Tebaldi as

Leonora. Warren had just sung his big aria, 'Urna fatale del mio destino', and was about to launch into the vigorous *cabaletta* that follows it when he staggered forward, in full view of the audience, and fell. Tucker rushed in from the wings crying 'Lennie, Lennie!'. The curtain was hastily lowered and, after what seemed like an interminable few minutes, General Manager Rudolf Bing came to the footlights to announce that the worst had happened: Warren was dead and the performance was at an end. Perhaps it is just fortuitous that that very year, serious discussions were taking place about the eventual move to a new house.

The old Met was a nineteenth-century building that survived too long into the twentieth. It had a wonderful, elegant, spacious auditorium. Designed on the classical European principle of a series of horseshoe-shaped levels, it gave singers and boxholders a wonderful rapport. It was a good house in which to sing, and a superb house, especially if you were in a reasonably central box, from which to see and hear. However, there were over 700 seats from which you could only see a fraction of the stage. I myself remember watching, for example, the left half of a *Lohengrin* and a *Così* and the right half of a *Cav* and *Pag* in the early 1960s, and standing through a wonderful *Turandot* designed by Cecil Beaton, starring Richard Tucker and Birgit Nilsson, and not being able to see the upper part of the multilevel staging. If the auditorium had problems, these were nothing to those backstage. The house was bounded by the limitations of a rectilinear New York city block and, before long, outgrew the space available. When Giulio Gatti-Casazza came as General Manager and Arturo Toscanini as Music Director in 1908, it was with the understanding that up-to-date facilities and, in time, a new house would be built. Dressing rooms were small and dingy, the stage machinery so primitive that it was becoming dangerous, and scenery and costumes had to be stored outside the building on Broadway and Seventh Avenue under makeshift and inadequate covering, falling prey to Manhattan's variable weather. Risë Stevens once told me how she sang the role of Carmen in a dress that was sodden as a result of a recent downpour.

The new Metropolitan Opera (designed by Wallace K. Harrison, the architect responsible for the United Nations building and the Rockefeller Center) was opened in 1966, and is the central, most prominent building of an arts complex, the Lincoln Center, that takes up four entire blocks just west of Broadway, between 62nd and 66th Streets. Opera thus moved uptown again, from 14th Street to 39th Street to 66th Street, paralleling the general uptown shift in the residential and cultural patterns of New York.

The Lincoln Center also houses two theatres, the Juilliard School of Music, a Library of the Performing Arts, two concert halls and the New York State Theater, home of the New York City Ballet and, during the season, the New York City Opera. The Center was inaugurated in the mid-1960s, yet nobody in New York seems to remember what the area was like *before* its transformation (if you want to know, see the movie of *West Side Story* and watch out for the dilapidated section of New York that flies past beneath the opening credits).

The Lincoln Center became the prototype for arts centres developed in many cities of America and elsewhere. In Washington and Los Angeles, in Adelaide, on London's South Bank, and at the Centre Beaubourg in Paris and countless small provincial arts centres around the world, the Lincoln Center provided the great example. In the carefully sculpted aesthetic compatibility of a number of different but closely adjacent buildings, and in its generous use of the spaces between, the Lincoln Center is a model of intelligent planning.

The Met's operatic neighbour, the New York City Opera, was founded in the 1940s and, for many years, performed in the former Shriners' auditorium, known as the City Center, on West 55th Street. Under the direction of Julius Rudel, the City Opera grew into a thrusting and imaginative company, often playing a bolder repertoire than the Met and uncovering a wide range of new American and foreign talent. Indeed, it was at the N Y C O that Domingo applied for an audition when he first came to the United States in 1965. Rudel remembers well the stunning impression Domingo made on him even before he opened his mouth. 'If this man sings half as well as he looks we've got a real winner,' he thought, and once Domingo began to sing, Rudel immediately decided to engage him.

Domingo sang a couple of roles in late 1965 at the old 'Mecca Temple' on West 55th Street, and, when the time came for the

NYCO to open its new house at Lincoln Center, it was partly with Domingo in mind that Rudel planned the opening night. The opera was to be the US première of *Don Rodrigo* by the Argentinian composer Alberto Ginastera—a large-scale work with literally hundreds of participants on stage and off, plus an orchestra containing eighteen French horns and twelve trumpets, some deployed backstage and others in various parts of the auditorium. As Rudel recalls, the title part—a handsome Visigoth king from eighth-century Spain—seemed almost to have been written with Domingo in mind. 'I immediately assigned this difficult part to Plácido—I might add, over the strong objections of some of my immediate staff who worried about his youth, his lack of experience, his "too lyrical voice" and so on and tried to persuade me to engage another tenor. Well, the opening night was a triumph and catapulted Plácido into immediate world recognition. The composer was present and moved to tears.'

Once Domingo was safely installed at the Lincoln Center as the star tenor of the State Theater, he inevitably had his sights fixed on the big building just across the plaza. And the people at the big building, just as assuredly, had their sights fixed on him.

The new Met is, in many ways, a traditional opera house. Architecturally, it is a large, marble, rectangular cube, with five high, glass-filled arches at the front. The outer pair of arches reveal (or, in practice, partially conceal) two huge, original Chagalls on musical themes, which are unveiled when the public is in the house. The auditorium contains a large proscenium stage, faced by rows of orchestra stalls and five curved tiers of seats. The seating and carpeting are of red velvet, the stage curtain old gold damask, and the whole thing is topped by a great chandelier. You approach this vast inner sanctum through one of the layers of richly carpeted foyer, perhaps ascending the generously-curved central staircase, maybe pausing for a drink of cool water from one of the inlaid marble fountains 'In Memory of Ezio Pinza'. It is interesting to note that while the walls of the Met, the programmes and even the backs of the seats all bear the names of benefactors, without whose tax-deductible gifts none of this would have been possible, the free, cool water is named for one of the great singers of yesteryear.

The Met's auditorium is enormous, yet does not feel excessively so. Singers of an older generation may tell you that in the old Met you had a much larger space to sing across, but they are mistaken. The length of the new auditorium is actually the same as the old, but, because it is wider, it *looks* and *feels* more compact. Audiences, too, are not too discomfited or distracted by the size of the building in which they are seated; although the architects decided to maintain the curved, horseshoe structure of the traditional opera house auditorium, they still managed to contrive that up and behind the great centre of each horseshoe are row upon row of well-upholstered seats, virtually all of which face reasonably squarely towards the stage.

The Met, like any opera house, has spots in which the acoustics are imperfect. The imperfections, such as they are, tend to take the form of the sound coming across as too 'live' — that is, bright nearly to the point of echo in some side seats. First-time visitors sometimes come away presuming the sound they have heard has been amplified. Anywhere in the house, even at the back of a section of seating under cover of the next layer, the sound tends to be brilliant, singers and orchestra (particularly winds and brass) being clearly audible. The old Met had a softer, more integrated sound, but singers were known to strain there. In the new Met, most can fill the spaces, certainly in the 'big gesture' end of the repertoire — *Trovatore*, *Tosca*, *Turandot* and the like — and if the more intimate, quicksilver subtleties of Mozart or Rossini tend to get lost, the Met's managers believe that patrons will feel compensated when the house eventually provides English-language titles. These will not be 'supertitles', projected above the proscenium arch as in so many other opera houses in America and elsewhere, for the Met stage is simply too high and, in any case, General Manager Joseph Volpe and Music Director James Levine have long considered them distracting. Instead, 'Met titles' will be made available in a low light on the back of the seat in front of you. If you can *see* what the people on stage are singing about to each other, the argument goes, it is amazing how much better you feel you can *hear* them.

Acoustics is an inexact science, and the greatest experts can make awful errors — notably in the Met's other main neighbour on the plaza. When Philharmonic Hall became the first building in the Lincoln Center to be opened, in 1962, it was found to carry the most dreadful and inadequate sound. In particular, everyone complained that it lacked bass. More than a decade later, and at unthinkable expense, the hall was radically restructured, its acoustical properties entirely refurbished, and reopened (under the name of the man who picked up most of the tab and was to die the very week the Met's 1994 *Otello* went into rehearsal) as Avery Fisher Hall. The new Met, opened in 1966, was more fortunate, but its founding fathers also had more foresight. They had travelled to Europe, to Germany in particular, where a number of opera houses were being built after the devastation of the Second World War, and they came back having learned lessons that, cumulatively, were to hold them in good stead.

They decided to commission an opera house that *looked* like an opera house. Opera, after all, was a traditional art form and most works required a proscenium stage with traditional scenery, sets, make-up and so on. They decided to retain the horseshoe shape of the auditorium (and even the visual suggestion that the seats are clustered into boxes) and to exclude hard angles from their design. This is one of the secrets of the Met's bright acoustic: everything is curved — not just the tiers of seats and the exterior of each of the 'boxes', but the uprights and top beam framing the proscenium stage, the swirling, lotus-flower discs of gold leaf that embellish the ceiling, even the wavy Congolese rosewood walls that enclose the auditorium. Everywhere sound is projected rather than absorbed.

Perhaps the most famous feature of the Met's auditorium is its many small chandeliers — spiky little clusters of light, like so many luminous snowflakes, delicately suspended from the ceiling far above. As the lights (so to speak) go down, the chandeliers go up, literally. They are raised up past four tiers of seating so as not to obscure anybody's view of the stage, and they stay up throughout the performance. In the early days, the audiences used to applaud this little technological marvel, but nowadays they take it in their stride. What the public never sees, however, is the even more remarkable sight of these crystal clusters being lowered into the semi-darkened auditorium before the audience is admitted — glistening spiders spinning themselves a web up which they will later climb in full view of 4000 bemused spectators.

There are, perhaps, two things wrong with the auditorium. The first is the bizarre sculpture that hangs precariously above the spare, old gold proscenium arch, looking like a length of perforated computer printout tape threaded through bent, spiky violin necks. A chastity belt, one friend of mine calls it. The second is that there are no proper side foyers or even exits, so the entire audience has to leave through the back of the auditorium, which means that there can be a slow crush after a performance. However (unless there were a flash fire), these are small discomforts for an audience to endure in a house that is so good at fulfilling its main task.

Quite how good it is only those who work backstage can really know. For a start, the Met has not one stage but five. On either side of and behind the main stage are three further full-sized stages, while the fifth is directly below it, and, on all five, entire sets can be pre-assembled to lessen the time spent changing scenes. Thus, in the Met's *Hoffmann*, for example (which uses all five stages), Luther's tavern sinks down below ground before your very eyes, giving way to a vision of Spalanzani's massively complicated nutty scientist living room slowly rolling towards you from its pre-set position on the stage behind the stage. In *Billy Budd*, the set — a larger-than-full-size replica of a man-o'-war of Nelson's time — moves upwards as the action shifts from quarterdeck to hold. The stupendous multilevel Café Momus scene from Franco Zeffirelli's production of *La Bohème*, with some 300 people in position, is rolled on to the main stage as Act I is rolled off, the transformation taking less than four minutes.

Below, above and behind the auditorium, the Met is a maze of spaces, small and large — the biggest being for the painting and storage of scenery, the smallest tending to be for the offices of the people who actually run the Met. Right there, at the Lincoln Center, the Met makes many of its own costumes and props, has its own wigmakers, swordmakers and so on, and an electrical department that oversees everything from the replacement of bulbs in the spidery chandeliers to the smooth running of Spalanzani's cornucopia of inventive bits and pieces in *Hoffmann* to the cleanly coordinated arrival of the Q E 2-sized see-through liner in the *Flying*

Dutchman. As in every opera house, the Met has more sets, costumes and props than it can easily store, and so, in the corridors of almost every floor backstage, you will come across packing cases marked 'Ballo Act I' or 'Rosenkavalier Act II' or racks containing assorted regal gowns and capes or street urchins' leggings and tunics. Strange though it may sound for an opulent, modern, purpose-built opera house, but the Met is already proving too small. Indeed, it was actually *built* too small. Its five arches were originally to have been seven, and, when economic realities forced the planners to reduce the breadth of the building, it was foyer, storage and office space that were sacrificed.

On the outer left-hand rim of the building, one narrow corridor above the next for some six floors, where you might have expected, say, a series of emergency fire exits or interval bars, there are the executive offices of the Met. Here, in tiny rooms like the compartments in a railway carriage, linked by the narrowest of corridors, sit the powerful people who make the big artistic, managerial and financial decisions, the operatic movers and shakers. You want to know who will be singing or covering such-and-such a role in the Met revival of this or that opera a year or two hence? What Domingo or Pavarotti or Renée Fleming or James Morris is down to sing next season or the year after that? What a major revival of this or that opera will cost at present-day prices or who will pick up the tab for the new *Butterfly* or *Boccanegra* or whatever else is being planned, and why there is no *Tristan* or *Cenerentola* in the Met's repertoire? What does maestro X cost, why doesn't maestro Y ever work at the Met, and why, for that matter, is maestro Z booked so often? Here are the people who know and decide, who soothe frayed nerves, issue and sign contracts, talk huge money and live in a permanently umbilical relationship with their phone and fax machines.

This is the domain of Joe Volpe, now General Manager of the Metropolitan Opera, but who was an apprentice in the carpenter's shop when he joined the company in 1964. Volpe thinks back to Domingo's début in 1968: 'I was the Master Carpenter at that time so was on the stage for almost every performance. So, although Plácido and I did not spend time having long conversations together, we saw each other a lot and there were times when he needed this changed or that changed. And then, as I moved up the Met administration, we came into contact more and more.' Today, Volpe says, Domingo is absolutely central to all Met planning.

The Met is a busy twenty-four-hour factory. Consider a typical two-day period during the season — a Friday and a Saturday, say. On the Friday morning, there is a rehearsal of *Otello*. The first scene will have been set up by the overnight stage crew after they have struck the complicated set of the previous night's *Bohème*. The new crew have *Otello* to contend with during the day, and then have to put in place the great rotating *Barbiere di Siviglia* set for the evening show. There is no stage rehearsal on Saturday morning, but the *Barbiere* set has to be struck and two performances set up during the day, *La Bohème* in the afternoon, and Cilèa's *Adriana Lecouvreur*, perhaps, or Poulenc's *Dialogues of the Carmelites* in the evening.

If you could spirit yourself backstage at the Met on any Saturday during the season you could witness a miracle. The matinée opera is always broadcast, bringing additional pressures to bear on those involved. If it is a bulky, four-set opera (*La Gioconda* or *Hoffmann*, for example), the scene-change logistics are complicated, but must not run behind schedule. Then, as the *Gioconda* or *Hoffmann* sets, props and costumes disappear to their appointed places after the show, and those for *Arabella* or *Carmen* or *Stiffelio* emerge for the evening performance, one observes not just a busy theatre at work but, it almost seems, a military manoeuvre or, perhaps, to choose a more appropriate metaphor, a piece of massive balletic choreography. How the hundreds of chorus and non-singing 'supers' find themselves in costume and ready to go on in a big production like *Turandot* or *Bohème*; how none of them gets swallowed up by the massive hydraulic elevators that transport huge sections of scenery up and down several storeys of backstage; how some seventy people all manage a quick costume change on cue in *Death in Venice* (and the principal tenor effects one of his in seven seconds flat); how Hoffmann and his cronies survive as Luther's tavern is literally crushed underground by Spalanzani's fantasmagorical scientific wonderland; and how that wonderland, or great chunks of Peking or Paris or the forestlands or godly abodes of Wagner's *Ring*, are assembled offstage and then on, seems incomprehensible to an innocent observer.

To the stagehands, though, it is all fairly straightforward, if hard work. They enjoy making order out of chaos, and a complicated production like *Bohème* or *Die Frau ohne Schatten* can give the people who shift and shape it a great deal of satisfaction. Their favourites, though, not surprisingly, are the operas with the simplest sets, particularly one like *Wozzeck* (one of the few legacies of the old Met to have survived into the 1990s), which is simple yet aesthetically pleasing.

If you like big, expensive productions, every trick of stagecraft imaginatively used, split-level scenery, painted gauzes that appear and disappear, trapdoors, realistic or even real fires, men who descend from the heavens, women who walk on water, the whole encompassed by one of two vast cycloramas 270 feet wide and over 100 feet high (82 by 30 m), the Met's the place for you.

The Met is a big building. The Lincoln Center is a vast complex. If you walk fairly briskly, the Center takes ten minutes to walk around or fifteen if you are more leisurely about it. From Broadway it all looks beautiful and extravagant, a series of well-spaced buildings of bright travertine marble, each with its own distinctive style, yet each blending with the whole. From the Amsterdam Avenue side, however, you can pass by the Center and scarcely be aware of its existence. On the far side of the avenue are high-rise housing projects and a couple of schools, and on the Lincoln Center side, a large marble monolith broken by the occasional car-park entry and also, a little way above street level, by a small row of inconspicuous rectangular windows rather like those on the side of a small airplane — hard to look out of, impossible to see in. These, though you would never guess it, are the windows of the principal artists' dressing rooms at the Metropolitan Opera. Each room has a piano, a shower and toilet (facilities had to be shared in the old house), each is supposedly sound-proofed, and in each the sometimes severe house air-conditioning is turned off. If you *could* peer through the little windows, you might catch a glimpse of Luciano Pavarotti, Cheryl Studer, Kiri Te Kanawa, Samuel Ramey or Thomas Hampson changing, putting on make-up, singing scales, fielding telephone calls. Or perhaps of Plácido Domingo, face blackened, his gleaming Act I armour being given a final sheen, as he prepares to go on as Otello.

As Otello at the Met.

Rehearsing *Otello* at the Met.

'Put down your swords!' (*Above*)

Domingo and Carol Vaness rehearse the 'slap' (Act III). (*Below*)

Domingo and Carol Vaness in the love duet (Act I).

Otello confronts reality.
(*Left*)

Domingo and Elijah
Moshinsky come
offstage together.
(*Below*)

With Paul Plishka
(Lodovico) and Sergei
Leiferkus (Iago)
rehearsing Act III
(*Bottom*)

Domingo being made up for his first entry in *Otello*.

Backstage with *Otello* conductor Valery Gergiev.

With stage director Elijah Moshinsky.

Carol Vaness and Sergei Leiferkus chat to Met prompter Joan Dornemann during a break in *Otello* rehearsals.

Otello

— public (Act III);

— private (Act IV).

The Act III Monologue.

The opening chords of *Otello* are loud and fast; the closing chords subdued and slow. The blood races at the beginning and thickens at the end. This is tragedy on an epic scale, and perhaps the greatest union of plot, character, words and music ever created. Verdi, then well into his sixties, had not created a new opera since *Aida* in 1871, and needed a lot of subtle wooing and persuading by his publisher, Giulio Ricordi, before he would agree to consider composing once again. Ricordi, at a dinner party at Verdi's apartment in Milan in 1879, steered the conversation around to the kinds of plots that would work well as operas. Shakespeare's *Othello* came up as a splendid example, a play used many years earlier by Rossini. Verdi admired Shakespeare above all other dramatists, had long ago set *Macbeth* as an opera and, for nearly forty years, had nursed a frustrated desire to create an opera based on *King Lear*. As it happened, said Ricordi, the young poet and composer Arrigo Boito had ideas about how to adapt *Othello*. Would the maestro be interested in seeing Boito's scenario?

Within three days Boito had sent Verdi his *Otello* scenario. It was an excellent piece of work, but Verdi would not be cajoled. By all means put your ideas into a verse text, he told the young man encouragingly. It will always be useful — for you, for me, perhaps for someone else. In a string of letters to Ricordi, Verdi insisted that, as concerned their 'chocolate' project, as they nicknamed it, he was committed to nothing.

18 July 1879
Giuditta [Ricordi's wife] has written . . . about the chocolate, you write to me about the cocoa . . . Listen well . . . I warn you that I have not made the slightest commitment, do not want to make any, and that I wish to keep all my freedom . . . Do you understand?

23 July 1879
As for the chocolate and the cocoa, consider them jokes . . .

Verdi knew when he was being manipulated. In another letter to Ricordi he wrote:

4 August 1879
A visit from you will always be welcome in the company of a friend, who now would be Boito of course. Permit me, however, to speak to you very clearly and without ceremony about this

matter. A visit from him would commit me too much, and I absolutely do not want to commit myself . . .

If you come here with Boito now, I shall inevitably be obliged to read the finished libretto he will bring along with him.

If I find the libretto thoroughly good, I'll find myself committed in some way. If I find it good and suggest modifications which Boito accepts, I'll find myself committed even more.

If I don't like it . . . it would be too hard to tell him this opinion to his face!

No, no . . . You have already gone too far, and we must stop before gossip and annoyances arise . . .

Verdi considered himself retired, a country gentleman who had performed the state some service and deserved a measure of tranquillity in his old age. In 1881, he revised an earlier opera, *Simon Boccanegra*, and, a couple of years later, issued a tightened version of *Don Carlos*, but he repeatedly told everyone that he had no intention of composing anything new. Throughout these years, press gossip periodically suggested that Verdi was preparing an *Othello* opera. He himself had suggested to the baritone Victor Maurel that he might write 'Iago' for him one day, and Maurel would have been less than human not to have mentioned this to friends and colleagues. But Verdi was not amused. 'Why talk about an opera that doesn't exist?', he wrote petulantly to Boito.

Ricordi and Boito did not give up. In effect, a benign conspiracy was established between Ricordi, Boito, the conductor Franco Faccio and Verdi's wife, Giuseppina. It would do the old man good to have a new project, but he mustn't feel himself pushed. In 1883, Richard Wagner, his exact contemporary, died. Then nearly seventy, Verdi was incomparably the most famous composer in the world.

It was not until late 1884 that Verdi finally settled down in earnest to the task of setting Boito's text, and he and his young librettist corresponded vigorously about the details, adding here, adjusting there. The two men followed Shakespeare closely, though the play was inevitably tightened because words take longer to sing than to say. Thus, *Othello* contains some 3500 lines, *Otello* under 800. The greatest curtailment is that Verdi and Boito decided to cut out the whole of Shake-

speare's first Act so that, instead of beginning in Venice and seeing
Othello called before the Doge and Senate, explaining his relationship
with Desdemona and being summoned to lead the Venetian fleet
against the infidel Turks, we start on the shore of Cyprus as that battle
rages out at sea.

Otello had its première at La Scala, Milan, on 5 February 1887.
Conducted by Faccio, it was a triumphant success. At five the following morning, the crowds were still outside the composer's hotel
crying, 'Viva Verdi!'. Verdi, then seventy-three, was fêted like a
conquering hero as all Italy celebrated what was generally assumed to
be his last opera.

No opera begins more dramatically than *Otello*. There is no overture,
no scene-setting orchestral prelude, not even a page or two of atmo-
spheric chords. Instead, a rapid upbeat scale representing lightning is
instantly followed by a crash of orchestral thunder, and the storm that
is to end four Acts later with the calm of eternal death is already
underway.

Within minutes, after this initial choral and orchestral outburst,
the tenor strides on to deliver his triumphant opening exultation: a
mere dozen bars in which he is presented with the chance to dazzle,
like a flashing sword of tempered steel, and to set his mark upon all
that follows. As Otello glad-hands his way off stage again, the people
of Cyprus proclaim a famous victory, warming their spirits with the
fires that blaze in the harbour and on the quayside, then from the
alcohol that Iago proffers to all in general and Cassio (Otello's deputy)
in particular. Iago, so bluff and plausible, misleads all with whom he
deals, and soon succeeds in getting the drunken Cassio into the thick
of a dangerous brawl.

'Remember *why* Iago says he's giving out drinks.' Elijah Moshinsky, the Australian-born, British-based director who has been
engaged to direct the new Met *Otello*, is rehearsing the chorus. 'It's
the wedding night of your new commander and his bride. They're up
there [he nods towards a balcony atop one of the great Renaissance
buildings erected on the Met stage] doing you know what!' The
members of the Met chorus laugh at Elijah's elegant smuttiness.

'So, think what Iago's saying when he proposes the toast to Otello and Desdemona. It's a very two-edged toast and there must be an element of tin-cans-tied-to-the-getaway-car to your actions and expressions. OK? Right. Let's go back to the beginning of Iago's drinking song.'

Moshinsky is constantly on and off stage trying to cajole his chorus to act, and react. At the 'Esultate!', as they thrill to the arrival of their victorious leader, he reminds them that this is the first time they have ever seen Otello: 'You've heard of him. You've heard *about* him. You've seen his wife, who came to Cyprus ahead of him, and you've seen the battle going on out at sea. But you don't quite know what was going on in that battle or the details of its outcome. So, when the great man finally arrives, you're overwhelmed at his news and at his energizing presence.'

The chorus is always having to do *something*. When the various members warm themselves from the fires that are blazing, they are to react to the heat—covering their eyes, clutching their cheeks, turning away slightly, perhaps. In the scene where Cassio gets drunk, Moshinsky wants them to sway backwards and forwards with the music, as though representing the disintegrating view of the world as seen by the man who is drinking too much. In the third Act, the chorus has to behave as though at a great formal ceremony, shrinking away almost involuntarily, as Otello, who has just committed a great social blunder by insulting his wife in public, lurches among them. Moshinsky carries with him a copy of the original *Otello* production book (which dates back to the work's 1887 première) and one day reads out to the chorus the following all-important passage:

> The producer must . . . explain very clearly to the Chorus that they must not appear as an insignificant mass of people, but that each of them assuredly represents a character and must act as such, moving on his own account, according to his own feelings, preserving with the others only a certain unity of movement in order to ensure the best musical performance. Immobility, at least that not expressly desired in the production book, must be *absolutely* forbidden.

The new Met *Otello* is a difficult assignment for Moshinsky, for he was not the first choice as producer. The production was originally mooted some four years earlier as a major event to mark Domingo's twenty-five years at the Metropolitan Opera. Each season, the Met, like all opera houses, unveils a number of new productions, and several were scheduled for 1993–4. Three were of operas by Verdi, and of these, two had never been seen at the Metropolitan before: *I Lombardi*, which was to star Pavarotti; and *Stiffelio*, in which the name part, a Protestant pastor tortured by his wife's infidelity, was to be performed by Domingo. The third new Verdi production, also created for Domingo, and also featuring a middle-aged husband in agony over what he believes to be his wife's adultery, was *Otello*. Over the years, new productions of *Otello* had been mounted for Domingo at all the other major international houses: the Vienna State Opera, Covent Garden, La Scala. Now, at last, there would be a new showcase for his greatest role at what had become his 'home' house.

As soon as Domingo himself had put the dates firmly into his diary, back in 1990, the Met appointed the British team of movie director John Schlesinger to produce and William Dudley to design. Domingo was delighted. He still talks with affection about the Covent Garden *Hoffmann* Schlesinger directed him in back in 1980 (and British operagoers will also recall Schlesinger's richly evocative *Rosenkavalier* a few years later). A Schlesinger *Otello* was an exciting prospect, and the Met then went on to contract one of its star sopranos, Carol Vaness, to sing Desdemona in the new production, and Valery Gergiev, artistic director of the Kirov Theatre in St Petersburg, to make his Met début conducting the piece. A little later, it announced that the Iago was to be one of Gergiev's most distinguished Kirov colleagues, the baritone Sergei Leiferkus.

In April 1993, less than a year before opening night, the Schlesinger-Dudley production was cancelled. It seems their set designs were simply too ambitious — unworkable in a house that has to put on seven performances a week, including two on Saturdays. An alternative production team had to be found, and fast. Moshinsky, who had produced a new *Otello* for Covent Garden back in 1987 (also for Domingo), was approached. Would he be willing to come to the Met's rescue and undertake a new production of *Otello* at short notice?

Moshinsky, born in Melbourne and Oxford-educated, had made his name with a simple and direct *Peter Grimes* at Covent Garden in 1975. It was possible to produce grand opera economically with no loss of impact, said the critics in wonderment. Indeed, the clarity and simplicity of the *Grimes* production, they felt, enhanced its impact. It was a great boost for Moshinsky, but not without its hazards. The label 'Cheap, simple, but powerful' was a heavy tag for the young man to wear, one he was henceforth expected to live up to wherever he went.

Before long, the call came from the Metropolitan Opera, New York. At the time, the Met retained, as Director of Productions, the British director John Dexter, working alongside Music Director James Levine. Dexter, knowing that Moshinsky had worked as Assistant Producer on a new Covent Garden *Ballo in Maschera* and aware of his triumph with *Grimes*, invited him to the Metropolitan to direct a new *Ballo*. The resulting production, '*Ballo* in a box', was regarded unfavourably by New Yorkers as an austere, 'Brechtian' interpretation, a far cry from the lush, Zeffirelli school of production to which Met audiences were accustomed, and it would clearly be a while before the Australian wunderkind would be invited back to the big house in the Big Apple.

Over the next few years, Moshinsky built up a string of successful productions — in the UK, Australia and elsewhere — and in 1987, was entrusted with Covent Garden's centenary production of *Otello*, starring Domingo. This was originally scheduled for the previous season, with Peter Hall directing, but had to be postponed when Domingo, in the wake of the 1985 Mexican earthquake, cleared his diary of virtually all his operatic engagements in order to concentrate on raising money for Mexican relief.

Moshinsky's Covent Garden *Otello*, with set designs by Timothy O'Brien, placed the opera in a sumptuous late Renaissance palace — more cathedral than castle, with chequerboard flooring, tall Corinthian columns and décor *à la* Veronese. 'Traditional, yet imaginative', was the verdict of the critics, and Moshinsky was now encumbered with a new tag.

As opera directors became more and more daring, or outrageous, in their approach to hallowed works of the past, especially in Britain and Europe, many of Moshinsky's productions, particularly of Verdi, came to be widely regarded as havens of traditional respectability. While David Pountney at English National Opera bathed Verdi's *Macbeth* in green blood and had Lady Macbeth sing an aria from a bed suspended at forty-five degrees from the ceiling, Moshinsky gave Covent Garden a 'cheap, simple but powerful' version of the same composer's *Attila*, and, while preparing a picture-book *Stiffelio*, wrote an article in *Opera* magazine pleading that, of all composers, Verdi should be played 'straight' with no ironic commentary from the director, no alienating devices coming between the audience and the immediacy of Verdi's message.

Thus, when the Metropolitan turned to Moshinsky to rescue their scheduled 1994 *Otello*, they felt they were on more secure ground than when he had first been invited nearly twenty years previously. Indeed, Moshinsky, booked to produce a new *Ariadne* at the Met, was already working with the house so, in many ways, his were the ideal hands in which to entrust the reins of *Otello*.

It was a late call, but Moshinsky agreed, and quickly teamed up with designer Michael Yeargan and costume designer Peter J. Hall (who had designed the costumes for the Covent Garden *Otello*). All three were conscious that this was too great and profound an opera to do in a rush, yet very difficult to think through afresh in the limited time available. They were labouring against another disadvantage, too, as their show was to replace a much-loved production by Franco Zeffirelli, dating back to the early 1970s (and which Met audiences knew they were seeing for the last time when Pavarotti sang Act I at the September 1993 Gala). Vast, craggy, the Zeffirelli *Otello* was full of crenellated, castellated walls, uneven flagstones and the spray of the sea as the bows of Otello's ship heaved into view — all the paraphernalia of richly romanticized late medievalism, a gorgeous, Gothic Cyprus of the imagination. Something of the effect can be gleaned from the movie of the opera Zeffirelli was later to make (though the operatic production, unlike the film, had the virtue of permitting the characters to remain reasonably motionless when singing of love or contemplating the eternal stillness of death).

A Moshinsky-Yeargan *Otello* would certainly be different. Different, at least, as far as New York was concerned, for inevitably, perhaps, the Renaissance palace setting, familiar to Covent Garden audiences, was to reappear, albeit in grander form, when the new *Otello* was unveiled at the Met in March 1994.

'Put down your swords!' calls the commanding voice of Otello, aroused from his nuptual bed by the courtyard brawl. Thus far, the man singing Otello has had almost nothing to do—except stride on stage, not once but twice, and, on both occasions, deliver a highly muscular vocal fanfare of stentorian power and authority.

'What's going on here?', he asks as the fighting stops, instantly, on his command. 'Are we stooping to the level of the Saracens we have just defeated that we behave like this?' He turns to Iago— 'honest Iago' in the opera as in the play—for information: 'I, I don't know', Iago answers sheepishly, confident that Cassio will shortly be blamed for starting everything. Desdemona appears in the background, disturbed by the fracas. Otello turns tenderly towards her, then rounds on Cassio, and instantly demotes him, much to Iago's almost uncontainable delight. As all but Otello leave the stage, Iago doubtless reflects how easy it is, in a world populated by people who *are* honest, to dissimulate, plot, conspire and destroy.

Otello the clarion commander is replaced by Otello the lyrical lover as he and Desdemona embrace slowly over the tender throbbing of the lower strings in Verdi's dark, velvet orchestra. This is virtually the only love duet in all of Verdi's operas in which the participants genuinely believe themselves to be absolutely trouble-free, and the black general and his young white bride kiss each other gently and sing of their mutual love in words and music of surpassing beauty, gazing into each other's eyes and the starry heavens above.

'My interpretation of the role has to adjust, to some extent at least, according to who my partners are,' says Domingo, 'and who is directing. When you have done the opera nearly 200 times, the most difficult thing is to find new aspects of the role. So it is important for me to work with a good director and together to try to look for something new, something different.' In some productions, the producer has wanted him to appear palpably Islamic, with a sword in the final scene that is curved, like a scimitar. This has served to emphasize Otello's 'otherness', his sense of being

130

rejected because he is culturally alien. Other directors have built in a suggestion that Iago, a 'man's man', is in some way homosexually attracted to his leader — something that certainly does not appear in either Verdi or Shakespeare, but which might help explain not only Iago's cold indifference to Desdemona, but also his fury when Otello grants preference to Cassio.

How black should Otello be, and how old? 'In the Zeffirelli film,' Domingo recalls, 'Franco wanted me to look very black, very African, not just in my skin colour and hair, but also in my movements and facial expression. You could see, just before the killing of Desdemona, that he was clearly going back to his African roots. In other productions, Otello can be scarcely darker than a European.' The point is that Otello regards Desdemona, Iago, Cassio and the rest as being somehow people of the same race, the same culture, and feels that he himself is an outsider. It is the same with Otello's age. When Domingo first took on the role, he was not yet thirty-five but he was conscious that he had to play a man close to fifty, which, during the time of the Venetian Republic, was quite old. Otello, he says, is anything from fifteen to thirty years older than Desdemona, and this difference in their ages is one of the things that worries Otello. Cassio, after all, is a young man of her own generation, her own *milieu*. 'If my Desdemona is, or looks, very youthful, mid-twenties, say,' says Domingo, 'then I try to appear not older than about forty. If she's obviously a little older, more mature, looking thirty-something, which I suppose is true of most of the sopranos I sing with, then I will try to look closer to my real age, early fifties or so.'

Domingo has sung *Otello* with every major Desdemona of the past twenty years — Katia Ricciarelli, Renata Scotto, Anna Tomowa-Sintow, Mirella Freni, Margaret Price, Kiri Te Kanawa — and, each time, the relationship is subtly different. Carol Vaness is tall, slim (she has lost a lot of weight during the previous year), with glamorous cat-like eyes and black, slicked-back hair *à la* Callas. A distinguished and versatile singer, Vaness took on all the female roles in the Met's most recent revival of *Hoffmann* (opposite Domingo), from coloratura doll to sensuous mezzo. Best known perhaps for her cool and beautiful singing of Mozart, Vaness is thrilled to be singing Desdemona with Plácido: 'It's like having the greatest seat in the house!', she enthuses.

Vaness has hurt her back, which was not made any better when she and Domingo rehearsed the final scene when he has to throttle her, then drag her across the floor towards the bed. The Met has booked not only the young Russian soprano Lyuba Kazarnovskaya as its official, paid cover for the role of Desdemona, but also the highly talented young American singer Renée Fleming to take over the role when the production is seen again later in the season. Both women are in the house at rehearsals, and, in Vaness' temporary absence, both get a chance to don the stately gowns and chestnut wig with which Hall has clad Otello's wife. Kazarnovskaya is tall, stately, with a voice that is strong, dark-hued, and slightly gutteral in the East European fashion, and Fleming is intensely lyrical, with a rare combination of power and vulnerability. One day, Domingo makes love to Kazarnovskaya in the morning and kills Fleming in the afternoon. Next day, Vaness is back. In Europe, where there is always likely to be an available Desdemona or Carmen or Aida available somewhere within two-hour flight range, many houses do not book (much less pay) an official cover; here, in the premier house of North America, there are two alternative Desdemonas in attendance.

Act II of *Otello* contains the one major element added by Boito to Shakespeare's play: a solo aria in which Iago spells out his credo. I believe in a cruel god, he laughs, and — especially shocking to nineteenth-century Italian audiences — that nothing awaits us after death. This is Machiavelli's cool Renaissance manipulator cross-fertilized with the nihilism of Boito's most famous creation as an operatic composer, *Mefistofele* — the very embodiment of pure evil, all the more so for never revealing so much as a hint of it except when alone (or with his wife, Emilia). In the play, Iago is jealous of Cassio's rank and also, perhaps, hopes to bed Othello's wife — motives that can serve, if required, for the opera, too. The real fascination of Iago, though, is, essentially, *what* he does and *how* he does it rather than *why* he does it. He is the consummate artist of evil. Thus, when Otello comes to join him on stage, we know that he is a fly about to be fatally enmeshed in Iago's web of calculated malevolence.

'Is Domingo all right?', whispered a concerned admirer in the darkened Met auditorium one morning as the rehearsal progressed. On stage, Domingo, dressed and made up as the Moor, slumped heavily into a chair, sighing, head in hands. His movements were uncharacteristically angular, impulsive, the blackened brow furrowed and pained. During an earlier scene with Iago, he had hardly looked at his baritone colleague while they were supposedly singing to each other, and he seemed permanently distracted. He would walk slowly, as though in pain — or else unnecessarily fast. Every now and then Domingo would glance over at the conductor and out into the theatre, blinking painfully, it seemed, in the bright lights. His eyes drooped heavily and his lower lip was exposed in a pout of pained resentment. The huge shoulders were even more hunched than usual.

Of course Domingo *was* all right — he was merely acting. A couple of hours later, backstage, he was chatting amiably to colleagues, making a telephone call or two, sipping a black coffee and preparing to go off with Marta for a late lunch.

Otello is merely one of many roles that Domingo undertakes. They are all different, and it is a common error to identify an actor with the parts he plays. However, every performer brings something of himself to the stage. Just as Meier in Vienna acknowledged that there were aspects of herself in the role of Sieglinde, so, presumably, there are elements in Domingo's personal make-up that contribute to the towering portrayals he is able to give of Canio, Cavaradossi, Hoffmann, Don José, Siegmund, Gustavo and — above all, perhaps — Otello. This, certainly, is the role with which he has pre-eminently become associated. By the time of the new Metropolitan Opera production in March 1994, a Domingo appearance in the title role of Verdi's great masterwork had long become considered the very pinnacle of operatic art. 'Plácido Domingo *is* Otello', said an ecstatic Joseph Volpe, General Manager of the New York Metropolitan Opera, after the triumphant first night — 'or, rather, Otello *is* Plácido Domingo!'

There does seem to be something in the role that holds a particular attraction for Domingo, and it is certainly one that he approaches differently from all others. 'There is no doubt that *Otello* requires everything from me,' he reflects, commenting on the huge dynamic range, the widely different lyrical and dramatic passages the title role encompasses, and the immense psychological demands of the role. It is the Everest of tenor parts, he says, the marathon, to be treated with special respect. 'I will never sing *Otello* one night and then, a few nights later, do something else, and then back for a couple of *Otellos*,' he says. 'I always want, when I am singing *Otello*, to feel that this is a special occasion, that the production is an important one, that this is something I have specially been looking forward to. And I never want to feel, "Oh my God, I've still got a couple of *Otellos* to do before I can go off and get on with something else". No. *Otello* has always to be a special occasion for me.' Why is he so drawn to this part? Are there perhaps elements in Domingo's own make-up that he is able to call upon to help him flesh out this complicated character so convincingly?

On the face of it, the two men — the fictional character and the performer who so often embodies him — are very different. Otello, a black man in a white world, is only briefly a man at one with himself. As the opera starts, he is in the thick of battle, and the military victory in which he exults as he appears on stage for the first time comes to sound increasingly ironic. His wedding night is interrupted by fighting among his own troops, and even the limpid tranquillity of the love duet at the end of Act I is punctuated by memories of military exploits and, towards the end, by a near fainting fit by a man who clearly has difficulty keeping in control of his own powerful emotions.

It is the greatness of Otello, but also his undoing, that he is a commander, a decisive man accustomed to having his wishes obeyed. He is not used to opposition, and when he encounters it, is not easily able to deal with it in a calm and rational manner. In Act I, when he comes out to stop the brawl among his followers, his inquiry into the causes — and the justice he metes out — are summary. As in the play (where he is described as 'rash, and very sudden in choler'), Otello jumps to conclusions on inadequate evidence, is easily wounded, and the impulsive anger that can attain victory over the Turks can also be turned too easily upon those who love him. He is susceptible to flattery, gullible to the guile of people more manipulative than himself. He is a man desperately seeking peace, but going about it in entirely the wrong way.

Domingo, by contrast, is a man who normally appears to be entirely at one with himself and his world, a model of inner tranquillity. His emotions are generally kept strictly under control, and Domingo's instincts are always to favour conciliation over confrontation, to restrain impulse, to defer a difficult decision rather than act precipitately. This is a man with immense powers of concentration who clearly enjoys immersing himself in a complicated piece of work, absorbing detail and adjusting his own actions in accordance with the exigencies around him. Courtly, courteous, a man of considerable personal dignity, it is hard to visualize Domingo flying off the handle with a burst of impulsive anger (and his portrayal of Otello, correspondingly, is of a man bitterly hurt who broods internally on his misfortune, burning with sorrow even more than anger, where earlier tenors like Jon Vickers or James McCracken would present an Otello already demented almost to the point of murder by the middle of Act II). Of course, Domingo feels some things strongly, and occasionally the dark eyes will flash, the powerful head will move close to that of his interlocutor, and something of the intensity that is so familiar from his stage performances will briefly pepper his private conversation. Genuine anger, though, is rare, and quickly forgotten. A search for compromise is soon initiated, and the storms of an Otello rapidly subside before the accustomed placidity of Domingo.

But the two men, the factual and the fictional, are not entirely unalike or the one would be incapable of assuming the mantle of the other. Both are middle-aged, tall, attractive and widely admired. Each is a man of action, an achiever accustomed to taking on ambitious and risky projects in full public view and generally succeeding. An aura of power and authority attaches to both, and each flourishes in lands far distant from his origins. Each, therefore, is, in one sense, an outsider at the scene of his greatest triumphs; a man who has adapted to and, in effect, conquered worlds to which he was not born. Each is constantly called upon to make decisions, often ones that he would find it preferable to avoid, and each has to fight hard to maintain the space within which to concentrate on what he considers his priorities. Both men, though powerful figures in a highly political world, are themselves transparently honest and inclined to believe in the straightforward honesty of those with whom they deal, and so both are capable of being hurt by less scrupulous operators.

Each, too, faces a conflict between the demands of his private and public spheres — on the one hand anxious to nurture and protect a stabilizing inner world of home and hearth, yet finding that this inner sanctum is constantly intruded upon by an ever-demanding external world to which, in some sense, he has allowed himself to be equally committed. Nowhere are the private and public conflicts of one man more painfully portrayed than in the third Act of *Otello* when, several times within a single line of music, the tortured Moor alternates between official utterance and hissed reprobation. 'Leave me!', he eventually calls out to the vast crowd towards the end of the Act, desperate to be alone.

Neither Domingo's personal style nor his domestic circumstances are, of course, remotely similar to those of Otello. Marta Domingo is *not* a generation younger than her husband or from an unfamiliar background or culture. For over thirty years, this highly intelligent and supportive woman has helped provide a powerful underpinning of strength and stability to her husband's peripatetic existence. However, there are many times when the intrusions of public upon private life must have proved irksome to Plácido, and when he must have been sorely tempted, like Otello, to dismiss the crowds of people that pursue him wherever he goes.

It is, perhaps, a vaguely perceived line of continuity between the ostensibly different personalities of Domingo and Verdi's Moor that especially attracts Moshinsky to the idea of, once again, directing the former to play the latter.

'Plácido probably feels he owns the part,' says Moshinsky affectionately, 'and he really does. He's a complete master of the role. But I have to hand it to him in that I think he really wanted to be stimulated by something new, something different. So we started to push it towards a whole different area.'

I asked him to explain. 'Domingo occupies a very important place in opera at the moment,' Moshinsky reflects, 'indeed, he's in many ways the most powerful person in the international operatic world. And yet he appears to be able to bring it off with a kind of easy charm, a generosity of character, always on an even keel with everybody — the tenor whom everybody loves. But it seems to me that this kind of permanently sunny persona can only be adopted at a price and that Plácido must be a more complicated person than he allows himself to appear.

'Every performer has a role where he can express a side of himself which he probably can't when he's not in make-up,' Moshinsky continues, and suggests that the part of Otello may fulfil this function for Domingo. 'Plácido seems to have almost an emotional need for this role, to delve inside it, as though it allows him to dig into parts of his personality that in his outward life he tries all the time to cover up. And I think that the difficulties that Otello faces, the destructiveness and *self*-destructiveness that are all part of the character—these are things that Plácido (like all of us) must have deep down somewhere, for I simply don't believe that anyone so outstandingly capable of portraying these darker, pained, tragic roles, and the ultimate nihilism of Otello, can be merely the permanently genial, supportive and sociable colleague we see in the opera house every day. Plácido *is* all these things, of course,' Moshinsky emphasizes, 'but not *merely* these things. And, strangely enough, just because the physical make-up required to perform Otello is so intense and he can't perform it as himself (he has to black up and, as it were, to dress up for it), I think this role could help him release a side of his own personality that he evidently needs to express. After all, the complexity of the character of Otello could never be so brilliantly recreated without what I am convinced is the complexity within Plácido himself.'

Moshinsky says he sensed from the outset that Domingo was keen to try to plumb greater psychological depths as they worked on the character together, and yet, certainly during the first week or so of rehearsals, Domingo was 'like a horse, shying away from something'. He was complaining, just a little bit, that this production was too much like that at Covent Garden, Moshinsky sensed, that he didn't think this or that detail would work, that this was a special occasion for him, and so on. 'Then, something happened, there was a kind of switch, a moment of trust occurred.' From then on, as Moshinsky sees it, Domingo started to open himself up to the deeper recesses in his own character and became fully committed to the renewed attempt that Moshinsky offered to bring ever-deeper insights to the greatest role in all opera.

Moshinsky was determined from the outset to give this production a sense of psychological consistency, while constantly aware that Met audiences and patrons would also want to see a grand, spectacular production ('lots of golden flags and smoke'). So he set out with the idea of a central figure, Otello, who contains the seeds of his own destruction, and built up both the psychological and physical aspect of the production from this basic premise.

For a start, he says, Otello has married the wrong girl. Desdemona is clearly quite wrong for him — far too young and of a totally different race and social background. Thus, the marriage itself is both a symptom and a cause of Otello's tremendous sense of personal chaos and confusion. So Moshinsky and his cast worked on the Act I love duet, for example, not just as an affirmation of love, but as a kind of duet between a flawed older character who is constantly healed by the presence of an innocent, young girl. 'But the girl is *too* innocent for him,' says Moshinsky, 'too young, too inexperienced — so, even if you didn't have Iago, the marriage would still have collapsed. The destruction, the violence and eventual death come, therefore, not from Iago but from within Otello himself.'

It was this premise — that the mayhem of the final Act ultimately emanates, not from Iago, but from Otello himself — that informed the entire production. There *were* plenty of golden flags and smoke in the production, an entire battlement wall that sank down to stage level after the opening chorus, and vast Corinthian columns and Titianesque wallcoverings of positively cathedralic proportions. But Moshinsky was also aiming at a sense of psychological unity and consistency, calling, above all, on the great wells of emotion that he was convinced lay deep in the psyche of his principal performer.

It is in Act II that some of the more destructive aspects of Otello's personality begin to reveal themselves as he comes on stage in the wake of Iago's 'Credo'. Otello is a successful general and, now, a political administrator, and Domingo likes to portray him looking at maps, documents that need signing, and the like (in the Met production, he is provided with a large map of his own homeland,

Spain). 'I like to be busy when I come on in this Act,' Domingo explains, 'and not look my Iago in the eye too much.' Here, too, a great deal depends on whom he is playing opposite: 'Iago shouldn't be too obviously evil,' he says, 'otherwise Otello will later appear foolish to have believed him.' The best Iago, he says, is someone who appears to be bland, respectful, and entirely plausible — the loyal lieutenant. This way, Otello can gradually be taken in by the deference he is shown, and by Iago's feigned reluctance to inform him of his suspicions.

Sergei Leiferkus agrees. Iago should wear very soft boots in Act II, he laughs: 'He must seem a peaceful man, with gentle movements on stage — like a cat. His portrait must be pastel.' Then, in yet another graphic metaphor: 'Iago's a fisherman, he's fishing — never quite knowing what results his little attempts will come up with.' And when Iago begins to catch Otello on his baited hook, he must be genuinely surprised.

Thus, the opening scene between the two men in Act II, shortly after Iago's 'Credo', should be almost casual, as though the junior man is trying, with some difficulty, to get his boss' attention for something that is difficult to broach. Cassio and Desdemona have just been seen talking together, which Iago pretends to find significant: 'Did Cassio know of your love for Desdemona when you were first wooing her?', he asks. Indeed he did, Otello replies, and sometimes acted as an intermediary between us. Why do you ask? Don't you think Cassio is honest? 'Honest?' echoes Iago, without answering the question, and goes on to warn his hitherto totally unjealous master about the green-eyed monster jealousy.

The seed has been sown, and Otello struggles with mixed feelings as he watches from afar an innocent presentation by the good folk of Cyprus to Desdemona, the attractive and popular young wife of their new governor.

Once injected with the poison that is to bring about his eventual downfall, Otello sees confirmation of his new fears in all that happens thereafter: 'Please forgive Cassio and reinstate him', Desdemona pleads, and immediately, this arouses Otello's suspicions. 'Not now,' he replies testily to her repeated entreaties, '*Not now!*' — and flings aside the handkerchief with which she tries to calm his agitated brow. Iago's wife, Emilia, picks up this most famous handkerchief in all literature, but her husband soon snatches it from her for his own nefarious purposes.

Otello is clearly on the rack: 'Rea contro me', he mutters, 'false to me', words which he still wants to disbelieve. Iago, however, is relentless. For the rest of this Act, says Domingo, and on until Otello's bitter outburst at the end of the Act III monologue, the tenor has to cope with perhaps the most intense and sustained passage — musically, vocally, and dramatically — in all opera. First, there is Otello's tragic realization that, if what Iago says is true, his whole life (the 'glory of Otello', he sings to a ringing top B flat) is, in effect, over. Then, from nobility to near panic, Otello turns angrily on Iago and almost throttles him, demanding proof of what he has suggested. In this production, he presses Iago backwards, painfully, down on to a table — 'I'm ruining everybody's back!', Domingo laughed one day as Leiferkus managed to pull himself up again after rehearsing this scene.

Iago, always respectful, tells the general how he overheard Cassio, in his sleep, talking to his 'sweet Desdemona' and saying tenderly to her what a cursed fate it was that gave her to the Moor. Of course, it was only a dream, says Iago, affecting nonchalance; nothing serious. But Otello's mood shifts from scepticism, anger and fear to something close to emotional paralysis as he allows himself to be tortured still further by Iago's offer of further 'proof'. Did you ever give Desdemona an embroidered handkerchief? With fruit designs? Yes, replies the Moor — like an animal cornered by a bright light, dreading what will befall him next. Yes, I did, it was my first token of love to her. Well, says Iago, plausible as ever, I think — yes, I'm sure — yesterday, I saw it in the hand of — *Cassio!*

At this, the Moor explodes with a tremendous outburst that leads to one of the most powerful, surging duets in all opera. Over heart-pounding *arpeggios* played by an orchestra following an increasingly agitated score, the desperate tenor and cynical baritone join forces in swearing a shared oath to the god of vengeance.

'You have to be able to master the voice,' Domingo says, 'it must not master you. And you have to be able, like a painter, to mix all your colours on the palette so as to be able to sing as lyrically or as dramatically as the moment requires.' However, if you are to sing the part of Otello successfully, he adds, face furrowed and serious as

140

though in character, 'the colour of the voice has to be dark. It doesn't matter if you are singing high or low, *pianissimo* or *fortissimo*. In *Otello*, the colour has to be dark, especially after Act I. If you don't have that dark, almost baritonal quality to the voice, you can't sing Otello.' As Domingo and Leiferkus link voices in the great duet at the end of Act II, 'Si pel ciel marmoreo giuro!', it is sometimes hard to distinguish the bright baritone of Leiferkus' 'honest Iago' from the 'heft' of Domingo's by now deeply anguished tenor.

The two men apostrophize the 'God of vengeance!' — 'Dio vendicator!' — while Gergiev whips up his orchestra to a foam of passion. As the curtain falls over the heavy, falling final bars, Otello — aghast at what he has just been saying — shrinks away from Iago, shaking his head slowly. The military hero who, on summary evidence, had impulsively demoted Cassio in Act I, has now sworn wrathful vengeance on that most innocent of creatures, his loving wife.

At early rehearsals, this overwhelming scene was carefully blocked for maximum effect. Domingo would throw off his purple, green-lined cloak at the outset of the duet and go down on one knee as he pronounced the initial oath. Leiferkus, affecting to enter the spirit of Otello's anger, would stand over Domingo to sing his first line ('Testimon e il sol ch'io miro'), and then the two men, singing together, would both stand — 'Not too symmetrically,' Moshinsky pleaded at one session, 'all you do by standing on each side of the prompt box like that is to draw attention to the existence of this strange piece of furniture in Otello's room!'. Domingo and Leiferkus would sing, if at all, in half voice, or an octave down, with only a piano in the huge Met orchestra pit. There was no point in the performers tiring their voices when it was the staging that was under the microscope.

Orchestra or piano, Gergiev was invariably there, conducting, watching, listening, observing, suggesting. A man of immense animal energy and personal charisma, Gergiev was always adding something. Sometimes Leiferkus would come to the edge of the stage and exchange a few words with his maestro in Russian — Gergiev, with his magnificently ravaged features, designer stubble and croaky, nicotine-stained voice providing a colourful contrast to his sedately dressed, soft-voiced baritone.

Gergiev has conducted *Otello* with Domingo before, with the Kirov in St Petersburg, and in Spain. Gradually, his characteristically urgent, surging, dramatic reading of the work weaves itself into the musical consciousness of all involved in the Met production. Does he feel superfluous at these stage rehearsals when Domingo and the others are only singing half voice, or marking? 'You never have half-voice rehearsals with Plácido,' he says, 'he is such a generous artist, always putting so much into whatever he is doing that when he's on stage, even if he is not singing out, you still have full "character" rehearsals.'

Moshinsky enthusiastically agrees. Domingo goes into a role, he says, the way an actor would, living inside the skin of his character whenever he is on stage, regardless of whether or not he is singing or in costume.

One day, a discussion started up as to how best to phrase that culminating phrase, 'Dio, vendicator!', with its high, powerfully sustained final note. Should the two men sing it in one breath? Should they sing in strict time (three beats for 'Di-i-o' then straight into 'vendicator') or, perhaps, insert a tiny pause before the second word? How long should they hold the final note? Domingo does not like the idea of slowing down the tempo, and therefore the intensity, of this final utterance, and, through a combination of mouthing and conducting, suggests with his whole body a taut rhythm to his two Russian colleagues. 'Di-i-o/ ven-di-ca-toooooor!' Gergiev mutters, trying out the rhythm Domingo suggests. 'Yes,' he says to his two singers on the stage above him, 'it seems to make sense.' 'Shall we sing it once,' Domingo suggests, 'just to fix it?'

At this, Domingo and Leiferkus come to the front of the stage, adopt their arm-raised positions and shatter the near-empty Met auditorium with an elemental appeal to the forces of darkness that is so powerful as to tempt the chandeliers up in the roof to part company permanently with their moorings.

In Act III, the knot tightens still further for Otello and his doom-destined wife. By now, the décor is all plum red—the lighting on the marble pillars, the Titianesque painting that provides the backdrop, the robe worn by Desdemona (in place of the whites and pale greens of earlier Acts). The colour of Empire. The colour of blood.

As Desdemona approaches, Iago reminds Otello quietly about the handkerchief (how could he forget?), and Otello's voice sinks to a low B as he prepares to confront her. She again pleads on behalf of Cassio, and is utterly taken aback when her irate husband demands to see the flower-embroidered handkerchief. Desdemona, of course, cannot immediately produce it and is thunderstruck by the outburst of anger to which she is subjected: 'You speak as though possessed by a Fury', the poor girl sings, uncomprehending, as the husband she idolizes accuses her of being a harlot (in a bitter phrase that rises to a briefly touched top C). Otello's anger towards her is now in danger of becoming not only verbal but also physical.

In a monologue of surpassing power, the great leader is reduced (as Domingo puts it) 'from anger to desolation', prostrating himself before a God who has brought him lower than the worm. *Any* affliction, Otello broods darkly, in the lower register of the tenor voice and scarcely moving off a single note, would have been more bearable than this. Domingo, crouching at the base of one of the great red columns, sings these lines with a voice bereft of colour or resonance, the sound of a man whose emotional vitality is close to extinction. Otello's wounded energies only revive at the thought of the death and damnation that he now knows are in attendance.

'Cassio is here!', calls Iago suddenly, out of nowhere, and the Moor, desperate for a resolution of his intolerable problems, cries out a bitter and heartfelt, 'Oh gioia!'. From the point of view of the tenor singing the title role, this great cry of joy, with its powerful high B flat, signals the end of the sustained intensity that began halfway through the previous Act ('I really do feel a sense of joy when I reach that phrase!', Domingo smiles). However, for the character he is playing, the torture continues without respite.

You hide there, says Iago, and keep watch on what happens. Iago then engages Cassio in trivial banter about their women friends, making sure Otello overhears the general drift, but not the detail. The famous handkerchief materializes (for Iago has placed it, as if it were a favour from an unknown admirer, in Cassio's quarters). The two men laugh crudely and Iago flashes the handkerchief playfully, ensuring that Otello will see it.

'How shall I kill her?', asks the Moor, charging forth like a bull from his hiding place the moment Cassio leaves. In bed, where she has sinned, Iago suggests, to Otello's grim satisfaction—at which point, an offstage trumpet fanfare announces what will be a further turn of the rack for Otello. Proclaimed as the 'Lion of San Marco' by his admiring followers, he is presented at a formal public ceremony with a letter by the Doge's representative, Lodovico, summoning him back to Venice and ordering that his place in Cyprus be taken by . . . Cassio.

'Bring Cassio!', orders Otello curtly, snarling bitterly at his wife all the while. 'We leave tomorrow.' He advances towards Desdemona and, shedding his last vestige of dignity, turns on her and humiliates her in public, sending her to the ground, in tears. In most productions, Otello grabs Desdemona's hands, and, in effect, wrestles her to the ground. Here, however, he slaps her face—the most offensive action he could inflict upon his fragile and sensitive wife. *Otello* may be the grandest of grand operas, big in emotion and gesture, but in this scene, as throughout, Moshinsky and his cast are keen to sustain psychological verisimilitude. Thus, Desdemona is not physically injured by the slap, but she is deeply stung mentally, and all who are watching are visibly appalled at what they have witnessed.

By the end of the Act, the 'Lion of San Marco' has completely lost control over himself, orders everyone to leave him, and mumbles to himself before collapsing in a fit of barely conscious exhaustion at the feet of his victorious tormentor, Iago.

The final Act takes place in Desdemona's bedroom. Attended by Emilia, she prepares for sleep, but, in an extended *scena*, Desdemona clearly fears death. When Otello enters, brandishing a sword, he kisses the sleeping form of his wife to the tender music of their Act I love duet. Desdemona, lying like a sacrifice on an elevated altar, awakens. Otello tells her to atone for her sins, then smothers her. Emilia rushes back in, hears Desdemona breathe her last and, in a matter of a mere two or three minutes, Verdi brings everybody back on stage for the final *dénouement*. Otello is rapidly made aware of the chain of mistakes that have led him to this dreadful deed. He swings his sword menacingly, then hands it over and, ultimately, regains the dignity that so distinguished him in earlier, happier times. 'Fear me not,' he sings slowly, to heavy, noble chords from the orchestra, 'for Otello is no more.'

He looks longingly and lovingly at his dead, innocent bride: 'a pious creature born under a malign star'. Then, perhaps in an effort to rejoin her, he finds a hidden dagger and stabs himself. To a final reprise of the Act I 'kiss' theme, he expires by the side of the wife he loved not wisely but too well.

The role of Otello is widely regarded as the pinnacle of the Italian operatic repertoire—the most difficult, yet most rewarding to perform, and one that Domingo has largely made his own since he first took it on in 1975. To many, the performances of Jon Vickers in the 1960s and 1970s were no less mighty—more muscular, more agonized, more demented, more brutally murderous. But it is Domingo's complete marriage of the musical, vocal and dramatic demands of this most challenging of roles that has crystallized it for a generation of operagoers as the acme of the operatic art.

Nowhere is Domingo more idolized than at the New York Metropolitan. Time and again, a packed audience will give him a standing ovation, with those in the upper tiers showering the stage with flowers and with the Met equivalent of ticker-tape—hundreds of bits of torn programmes fluttering down into the orchestra pit and on to the stage. A terrible mess for the Met cleaners to pick up the next morning, but a spectacular visible tribute for a great singer to receive after a highly acclaimed performance.

Many, of course, also want to see Domingo personally, to shake his hand or obtain his autograph. If you wish to go backstage from the Met auditorium after a performance, you have to walk down a series of long, narrow corridors, past the scrutiny of several layers of security, along another corridor lined with over a hundred tall, metal filing cabinets standing station over the approaches, and then, if Domingo is singing, there is a further security check as you are asked to line up and await your turn. 'Anyone who wants to see any artist *other* than Mr Domingo come this way please,' the guard will intone along the length of the line, 'all those who wish to see Mr Domingo kindly wait here in single file.' The line stretches round the corner and halfway back along the corridor with the metal cabinets.

To get this far, you have to be on someone's list. Every singer has a list of friends who have their permission to go backstage after the show. Met regulars who want to see, but are not friends of, the star have their names put on a list of some relatively minor cast member they *do* know, and thus gain easy access backstage (and can even jump the 'kindly-wait-in-line-here-for-Mr-Domingo' ritual). Otherwise, they simply leave a note to the star saying they would like to be on his list and no singer, certainly not a gregarious character like Domingo who knows the value of good public relations, is normally likely to refuse such a request. At most opera houses, even the most determined groupies are condemned to wait outside until their hero is ready to leave. At the Met, they can get right in alongside the genuine friends if they are determined enough.

Right in? Not quite. What tends to happen on a Domingo night is that the *real* close friends go straight to the Principal Tenor's dressing room, where Domingo will be changing out of his costume. A further small group, slightly less privileged, is allowed to congregate in the small anteroom that leads directly to the dressing rooms. Everybody else, and it can be a couple of hundred or more, must wait: 'Anybody who wants to see Mr Domingo please line up here!', the Met official will repeat, pressing people back along the corridor containing the filing cabinets. The crush to see Domingo is such that the dressing room area is quite inadequate as a place in which to receive, and the adjacent Green Room is often used instead. A table and chair are set up as another type of 'performance' commences.

Domingo emerges, costume and make-up gone and now immaculately dressed in suit and tie. 'How nice to see you,' he will smile, and 'How are you?' as he scribbles his name across yet another copy of this evening's programme. Someone will deliver a little speech: 'I heard you in this same role when you made your début in [such-and-such a house] in [nineteen-seventy-so-and-so].' 'Yes?', Domingo will answer courteously, summoning up as much interest as he can for the occasion. 'You were wonderful then, and you were even more wonderful tonight!', they say. 'Why, thank you so much,' says Domingo. 'Please write "To Lynda", with a "y",' says the fan. Another smile, another signature, another handshake or kiss, while

146

the people still lining up by the metal cabinets shuffle forwards a few feet closer to the packed Green Room.

Here at the Met — indeed, wherever Domingo appears — he is besieged by admirers after a performance, and it can be well over an hour before everyone who wishes has been ushered into his presence and out again. Some of the more private of today's singers hate this ritual and try to think of ways of avoiding or at least constraining and restricting it. After all, a performance can take a great toll on its performers and it is not everyone who, after four hours of intensive music-making, wants to endure a further hour or two of hero-worship.

Others obviously live on their adrenalin and at the end of a performance are still 'high' and so will take time to wind down. Domingo is one of them, excited, like a politician running for office, by the admiration of the crowds, and is cannily aware, as is a good politician, that big, happy crowds are good for business. Politicians like to believe, and they may not be entirely wrong, that everyone they shake hands with will be that much more likely to vote for them. There is magic in a touch, magic in an autograph, magic in the mystery of personal contact. Everyone whose programme Domingo signs, whose hand he shakes, whose cheek he busses, is a reinforced admirer. He knows this, and courts the backstage crowds accordingly. It is a good job he enjoys it, for it has so far taken up over 3000 hours of his life.

Monday 21 March 1994 — the first day of spring, although New Yorkers, emerging from one of the most relentlessly snowy winters in living memory, can hardly yet believe it. Three thousand miles west, in the auditorium of the Dorothy Chandler Pavilion in Los Angeles, the movie world will tonight pay homage to Steven Spielberg in the form of seven Academy Awards. In New York, the Metropolitan Opera will inaugurate the most eagerly awaited new production of its current season: *Otello* with Plácido Domingo.

Domingo, in town after a restful weekend, spends the day quietly at home with Marta in their apartment on Manhattan's East Side.

Like Otello, he does some desk work in the office upstairs, looking not at maps or state papers, but at the faxes that have come in. Everyone surrounds himself with appropriate insignia. Otello has his model ships, telescopes and crucifixes. Domingo's apartment contains a number of fine paintings (several of himself as Otello by Joan Marti), a host of medals, citations, honorary degrees and golden discs, plus a dazzling array of framed autographed photographs of many of the giants of the musical past, including composers (Rossini, Donizetti, Verdi, Wagner, Puccini, Strauss) and singers (among them Tamagno and Maurel—the original Otello and Iago—and, of course, Caruso). On one wall, there is a framed letter from the Mayor of San Francisco declaring September 15 1983 as 'Plácido Domingo Day', and there is a similar letter from the Governor of Connecticut a decade later. There are Domingo posters on display, not only of operas and concerts but also advertisements (including the famous 'Smoking Spoils Your Performance' for the American Lung Association), and the 1982 *Newsweek* cover that crowned Domingo 'King of the Opera'. Hardback books in many languages grace the white bookshelves, while a series of opulent and comfortable white sofas face glass coffee tables adorned with delicate metal sculptures and other *objets d'art*, many of them from Mexico. A pile of unanswered correspondence lies in one corner, but Otello doubtless had the same problem.

At five o'clock, Domingo leaves his apartment to make the short drive across town to the Metropolitan. He likes to get to the theatre early, especially for an occasion as important as this. He slips into the Artists' Entrance, smiles to the security people, and walks up past the army of filing cabinets towards his dressing room.

For his first entrance, Domingo will wear the shining armour Hall has designed for him, but, first his face and arms must be made up. Domingo usually grows a beard whenever he has a run of *Otello* coming up; he feels this helps give him the right air of dignity, and, perhaps, the age for the role. Should the beard be black or have flecks of grey? How curly should his hair be? Magda knows Domingo's hair well; she has been dressing it here at the Met for many years. 'How much foam do you think I should have?', he asks her. Otello is supposed to have come straight off a ship that, a moment before, was almost sinking in a tempest. 'I hate it when Otello looks as though he has just come from a parade,' Plácido laughs as Magda applies the foam.

'Ladies and gentlemen, *Otello* Act I will begin thirty minutes from now . . . half an hour to the beginning of Act I. Thank you.' The unmistakeably English accents of tonight's Stage Manager, Stephen Brown, come through the tannoy with his accustomed air of firm friendliness. If he says it is so, it is so. Plácido clears his throat, sits at the piano, and runs up and down a few scales.

'O K Victor, can I have my shower now?'. Seven minutes to go and Domingo's gleaming armour gets a final spray. By now, the tannoy is relaying the buzz of conversation from the audience. Plácido, hair foamed and armour-plated chest dampened, finally clanks his way from his dressing room forwards through to the stage and finds a space in the wings on stage left, alongside the ropes and gangplank that will be hoisted into place a few seconds before his entrance.

This is a Guild Gala night, with tickets appropriately priced. But the Met is a democratic house and a couple of thousand New York glitterati are augmented by another two thousand who simply love opera, *Otello* in particular, perhaps, and Plácido Domingo even more so, and who have managed to get themselves seats up in the Family Circle or standing places at the back of the orchestra stalls. There is a heightened sense of tension in the house as the lights go down, the chandeliers go up and Gergiev enters, to applause, to take his place at the podium.

Cr-r-r-r-ash! The explosion of *Otello*'s opening bars shakes everyone into rapt silence, and the magic takes hold. Domingo, in gleaming armour, strides down his gangplank straight from his naval battle to electrify his listeners, on stage and in the house, with Otello's opening exultation. The crucifix-embossed portcullis through which he has to exit lifts up precisely on cue. Leiferkus teases fellow soldier Roderigo with just the right level of *bonhomie*, scatters money as he invites everyone to have a drink, and grins with innocent joy as a playful child scampers between his legs, just as Moshinsky rehearsed them. The chorus and sword-bearing supers make maximum sound and fury during the fight scene and scudder to instant silence as Domingo emerges full of reprobation. For once, too, they all manage to get off stage, more or less silently, in time for the sensuous cello introduction to the love duet between Domingo and Vaness that follows.

Otello is not the longest opera in the repertoire, but it is assuredly one of the most economically written. From start to finish, there is no respite, no leavening, no 'boring bits' during which the audience, and the artists, get their breath back. Every moment in *Otello* has a dramatic and musical point — the perfect piece for a bundle of energy like Gergiev to conduct. During rehearsals, Gergiev occasionally disconcerted his players by his inclination to sculpt the music, to shape it rather than conduct it bar by bar. Sometimes, a particular passage would seem to go a little quicker or slower than usual, sometimes an all-important up beat did not appear to be given. Evidently, this was a 'dangerous' conductor, a high-risk merchant, not the safe time-beater that orchestras tend to be comfortable with. The result is that, on the night, the members of the orchestra watch him like hawks, responding to every gesture, every facial nod, every raised finger or elbow. Thus, the audience at the Met are treated to, if not one of the most lyrical or romantic performances of *Otello* ever presented, certainly one of the most dynamic.

Domingo himself, although so familiar with the work, performs the piece as though creating it for the first time. There is an integration of singing and acting that is little short of miraculous. At no point do the bodily rhythms either anticipate or lag fractionally behind the musical or vocal impulses, and the overall portrayal of greatness overthrown is simply heartrending. At the end of an evening of overpowering music and drama, the whole house rises in homage to the performers and producers and to the undoubted star of the evening, Plácido Domingo.

There is no Domingo 'list' tonight, no autographs-and-kisses ritual in the Green Room, no queue along the filing cabinets. Instead, Domingo, with all his colleagues, has a supper party to attend: the Guild 'bash', up on the Grand Tier level — surely the second most glamorous party to be held anywhere in North America that night. General Manager Joe Volpe rises to speak and the guests momentarily put down their Mousse 'Otello' and champagne to listen and applaud. Volpe has a few words of gratitude for everyone involved in the performance, from Gergiev, whose house début this is, to the much-loved tenor Charles Anthony (singing the small part of Roderigo) who joined the Met as long ago as 1954 and has given close to 2500 performances with the company.

Above all, he thanks Domingo, whom he frankly says he relies on, year after year, not only for performances of guaranteeably sterling quality, but for artistic advice, friendship and support of all kinds. When the record comes to be written of our times, says Volpe, Domingo is the one of whom it will be said: he is *the* operatic tenor. I don't believe anyone will ever achieve what he has achieved, he adds. People talk about the 'Golden Age' of opera, but future generations will look back to a night such as we have just experienced, and say: '*That* was a Golden Age'.

Domingo accepts the applause with a gracious smile and tells the assembled company how, for him, the Met is 'home'. He thinks back to his house début twenty-five years before, to his friendship ever since those far off days with people like Joe Volpe, Charles Anthony and the American bass Paul Plishka (tonight's Lodovico). He talks of the future, too, of new work lined up for him at the Met, including operas he has never performed before: Mozart's *Idomeneo* and Verdi's *Simon Bocanegra*. Volpe hints at projects planned up to and beyond the end of the century.

The new Met *Otello* did not completely satisfy all the critics — few productions of opera ever do — but most agreed with *Newsday*'s Tim Page who praised Moshinsky for a production 'that actually manages to combine spectacle with good dramatic sense', and Gergiev for conducting 'a surging, white-hot yet beautifully proportionate reading of the score'. America's premier opera company at its very best, he concluded. The *Wall Street Journal* praised the sets as 'exquisitely proportioned', while several observers praised Leiferkus for his suave, rakish Iago and Vaness for an especially touching 'Ave Maria' in the last Act.

Above all, however, praise was heaped upon Domingo, even by hardened sceptics. A 'phenomenon', Peter G. Davis of *New York* magazine acknowledged, whose 'voice has held up amazingly well over the years [and whose] musicianship remains impeccable'. Domingo, according to the *The New York Times*, 'has refurbished his voice at a time when it could be expected to show wear'. From the tempered steel of the 'Esultate!' to the bleak, baritonal 'voce soffocata' of the Act III monologue, the uncanny integration throughout of musical and dramatic intelligence, all served by the most heroic of voices—all these qualities were duly noted. 'One of the supreme operatic events in my experience,' concluded one grateful critic.

After over a quarter of a century at the top and nineteen years performing the 'Everest' of tenor roles, Domingo had clearly remained one of the greatest of all interpretative artists, and was still at the height of his powers.

4

'Fitzcarraldo' on the Rhine

PLÁCIDO DOMINGO, WITH ALTOGETHER OVER ONE hundred operatic roles to his credit, has been called many things in his time, most of them heroic and Italian-sounding. But on 5 June 1994, at the opera house in Bonn, crowned in a brilliant feathered headdress, he announced himself under a new name:

> Pery m'appella, in sua favella
> L'eroico popolo dei Guarany.

Il Guarany was first performed at La Scala in 1870, and was a triumph for its composer, Carlos Gomes, the 'Verdi of Brazil'. Pery, leader of the Guarani Indians in sixteenth-century Brazil, emerges from the rain forests, protects Cecilia (daughter of a local Portuguese hidalgo) from various fates supposedly worse than death, converts to Christianity and, as mayhem and destruction overtake most of the other characters, gets his girl at the final curtain as all else perish. Full of powerful tunes, often subtly harmonized and orchestrated, *Il Guarany* is an operatic extravaganza, containing many elements more familiar from works by Meyerbeer, Boito or Ponchielli (not to mention Verdi himself): lyrical arias and duets; a sweet, innocent soprano, heroic tenor and evil baritone; conspiracy and oath scenes, plus an exotic ballet and cataclysmic finale.

'*Guarany* is an opera I'd always wanted to do,' Domingo enthused during rehearsals, recalling his own Latin American background and the fact that many leading tenors of the past had sung the piece — Caruso, Gigli and, in the late 1940s, Mario del Monaco.

Enter Gian-Carlo del Monaco, the blue-jeaned, cigar-chomping son of the great tenor, and a distinguished operatic director who is now Intendant of Bonn Opera. 'My father always spoke warmly of *Guarany*,' said Gian-Carlo, showing me a photograph of Mario del Monaco as Pery from a production in Rio de Janeiro in 1949 wearing little more than a cluster of discreetly placed feathers. 'So when I got the opportunity to decide what operas to put on, this was near the top of my list—and I knew Plácido wanted to do it.' It was, indeed, Domingo's expressed desire to resurrect *Guarany* that gave the initial impetus to the whole project, but it was Gian-Carlo del Monaco who made it happen.

As del Monaco recalls it, he and Domingo had been working together in Barcelona and were having dinner one night. 'It was a warm evening, we had been eating well and perhaps drinking well.' Del Monaco sits back and draws on his cigar. He offers me a coffee. Delighted. Won't he have one? 'I *am* coffee,' he laughs, 'I have coffee in my veins instead of blood!' He sucks on the cigar again and sniffs a couple of times as though to clarify the memory.

'Plácido and I have been good friends for twenty years or more. The first time I directed him was in Caracas in May 1970 in *Adriana Lecouvreur*.' A few years later, the two men found themselves working together in major houses like Munich (*Cavalleria Rusticana* and *I Pagliacci*, *Manon Lescaut*), and more recently, they have collaborated on a number of productions at the New York Metropolitan (*La Fanciulla del West* in 1991, *Stiffelio* in 1993). At the Met alone they have plans to work together on new productions of *Simon Boccanegra*, *Butterfly* (which Domingo will conduct), *La Forza del Destino* and *Carmen*.

'So, Plácido's been a good friend for many years,' del Monaco reiterates. 'Indeed, he's godfather to my daughter. By the way— did you know he sang with my father?' It seems that the young Domingo sang Cassio to Mario del Monaco's Otello in a performance in Hartford, Connecticut, on 19 November 1962 ('the last time I ever sang a minor role', Domingo himself recalls).

When Gian-Carlo del Monaco became boss of the Bonn Opera, naturally he invited Domingo to sing there, and in June 1993, Domingo came to Bonn and performed *Otello* (the major role this time!). However, the two men had already planned a more historic collaboration. 'For a long time I had wanted to work with Plácido on something unusual,' del Monaco continues, 'so when we were at dinner in Barcelona that night I said, in a general sort of way, "Plácido, you know we really work so well together. We should do something really special together some time." Plácido nodded. "Something different," I added, "in Bonn ... Maybe something Latin American ...". That was all Domingo needed. "Gian-Carlo—let's do *Il Guarany*!", he exclaimed.'

Del Monaco remembers mentioning his plans to other opera managers, perhaps hoping to raise co-production money, but 'they all thought I was crazy and didn't want to know'.

Domingo, though, was delighted and salutes del Monaco's tenacity. 'It's easy to say that you'd like to do this opera or that, but to see an unusual and, in some ways, provocative idea through from that first spark, then solving all the practical artistic and financial problems and bringing it to the stage—that requires *real* courage.'

Del Monaco's filial piety and entrepreneurial flair, coupled with Domingo's hunger to conquer further operatic worlds, especially Latin American ones, gave the project a powerful impetus. Two further vital elements were required, though. The first was to find a conductor equally at home in Italian opera, German opera houses and the musical idiom of nineteenth-century Brazil. One man fitted the bill: John Neschling—born and raised in Rio, trained (under Hans Swarowsky) in Vienna, and steeped, since childhood, in the music of Carlos Gomes. And to direct this operatic extravaganza, del Monaco acquired the services of that celebrated *enfant terrible* of the German cinema, Werner Herzog, creator of *Fitzcarraldo* in which, you will recall, an obsessive operaphile, having glimpsed Caruso at the legendary theatre in Manaus in High Amazonia, supervises portage of a 320-ton steamboat over the mountains in his determination to bring opera to his own home town across the border.

'I first got to know Plácido in the late 1970s when I approached him to play the part of Caruso in *Fitzcarraldo*,' Herzog recalls. 'That didn't work out, but we have been friends ever since and have met many times, including in Bayreuth when I was directing *Lohengrin* and he was singing in *Parsifal*.' Neschling, too, has been a friend since *Fitzcarraldo* days. He has had an important career as a composer of film music (including that for *The Kiss of the Spider Woman*) and the two men had often expressed a desire to work together.

Thus, the 'dream team': a quartet of operatic conquistadores, assembled on the banks of the Rhine to mastermind the first major production in modern times of a work they all believed in, but that almost nobody outside their immediate circle of colleagues had ever even heard of.

Ask most people what they know about Bonn and two things will probably emerge: that it is the town where Ludwig van Beethoven was born and that it became the capital of West Germany in the wake of the Second World War. Beethoven's presence is everywhere: a great glowering statue stands in one of the city's pedestrian squares in front of an ornate building that turns out to be the central post office, while the house of his birth is preserved as an attractive and moving tourist attraction. The main symphony orchestra in town, which also plays for the Bonn Opera, is the Orchestra of the Beethovenhalle, the name of the concert hall in which it performs.

In Beethoven's day, Bonn was residence to the powerful archbishops of nearby Cologne, but for 150 years — from the time of Beethoven's departure for Vienna and the repercussions of the French Revolution in the late eighteenth century until the late 1940s — the city, despite the presence of an important university, became, essentially, a provincial backwater. Then, Konrad Adenauer, the wise old bird who was elevated in the wake of the War from Mayor of Cologne to Chancellor of West Germany, settled on the inoffensive nearby town of Bonn as capital of his new state. A 'federal village' was erected south of the fashionable suburb of Poppelsdorf to house the Government, while the old town centre, devastated like so many other German cities by Allied bombing, was gradually rebuilt.

Cultural life was not the first priority in a society wrecked by the nightmare of Nazism and war, and it was not until 1965 that a proper new theatre was opened in Bonn — a shiny, squares-of-metal-and-glass construction alongside the Kennedy Bridge, overlooking the Rhine. For twenty years this austere but efficient edifice was to serve the capital for opera, ballet and theatre. Then, in 1985, straight theatre moved to new premises and, henceforth, the house came to be used primarily for opera and dance.

The 'Oper der Stadt Bonn' may belong to the city, but it is far better financed than any normal municipal opera in a small town of some 300 000 inhabitants. Of its annual budget of DM 46 million (about £19 million), not much more than a quarter (DM 12 million, or £5 million) is recouped at the box office, with the remaining DM 34 million (£14 million) coming in the form of subsidy. Of this, 30 per cent comes annually from the coffers of the city and 70 per cent — that is, nearly DM 24 million (£10 million) — from the federal government.

The size and provenance of this subsidy have caused strong men to wilt, even in the well-upholstered world of international opera, and del Monaco is under considerable pressure to show value for money. When his contract began in 1992, he was told to build up a resident opera ensemble, engage fewer expensive guest stars than his predecessor and increase the number of performances (currently some 200 per season of 10 or 12 works). At the same time, the number of seats in the house was increased from 800 to a thousand by the addition of an extra tier, while seat prices for most performances have been kept well within the budgets of the good burghers (and rich diplomats and civil servants) of Bonn.

With a high subsidy and low seat prices, you might think that del Monaco has been given an easy job. Evidently not. It is hard to lure the diplomats up from the federal village to a house that avowedly emphasizes 'production values' and eschews pricey stars — particularly with the Cologne Opera, a major international house, just a short way down the Rhine. In his first season, del Monaco found himself severely excoriated for overspending by some DM 4 million, and he has had consistent difficulty filling the house. I attended a very creditable *Tosca*, for instance, one Saturday night (top price DM 90, or £37.50) and noticed many empty seats.

Furthermore, del Monaco's work is constantly beset by the shadow cast over every undertaking in Bonn these days: the decision made in the wake of German reunification to reinstate Berlin as the national capital and move all the arms of the federal government there by the year 2000. No restaurant, no hotel, no real estate or insurance company, no taxi driver or flower seller can be confident of surviving unscathed the exodus of people and money to Berlin that will culminate by the end of the century. Nor can an opera company, highly subsidized by a hard-pressed government that is scheduled to leave town.

These are substantial problems, but they may or may not have to be dealt with by the exuberant del Monaco, whose current contract lasts until 1997. He is a lively and imaginative Intendant, bubbling over with creative ideas most hours of most days. This is the man who brought rock bands into his opera house ('Why not? People like rock — and it brings in money I can put into opera!'). And, in addition to his own operatic productions at the house, he has also attracted a number of high-profile directors to Bonn — among them Ken Russell, Yuri Ljubimov and now Werner Herzog.

'I like to take things to the extremes,' Herzog said one day, in his quiet, courteous voice that often belies the content of his utterances. He was rehearsing the final scene of *Il Guarany*, where a fortress is blown up, killing everyone inside, a finale comparable to the destruction of the temple at the end of *Samson et Dalila* or of Valhalla at the conclusion of the *Ring*. Herzog and his designer, Maurizio Balò, had arranged for a vast iron portcullis, which has been hovering above the entire final scene, to crash down ferociously on to the stage, its spikes splintering on impact, while a flaming torch causes a massive explosion, after which huge chunks of masonry hurtle down from above — all accompanied by the most thunderous sound effects and dazzling flares. 'I want the whole audience to be literally blinded for a few seconds,' he adds, keen to take things to the very limits permitted by the ever-present municipal fire authorities. 'Aren't you afraid of dying?', someone asks in Herzog's movie *Cobra Verde*, and gets the cool answer, 'I haven't tried it yet'.

'When I made *Fitzcarraldo*, I had never been to an opera,' Herzog says, astonishingly. He claims to be musically illiterate, incapable of singing, playing an instrument or reading music. If he grew up with a musical centre of gravity, it was in early and Renaissance music, where he took to composers like Schütz, Victoria, Carissimi and (especially) Gesualdo. 'Wagner,' he laughs, 'was too modern for me!'.

Many of Herzog's films feature scratchy old recordings of vocal music, however. His television documentary about the courtship rituals of sub-Saharan nomads (*Wodaabe*), for instance, opens to grotesque images of men with their faces painted like women, and the sound of the last of the castrati singing Gounod's 'Ave Maria'; in *The Enigma of Kaspar Hauser*, about a teenage *ingénu* discovered on the streets of Germany in the 1820s who is 'civilized' by those who find him, the mood is capped by a primitive early recording of 'Dies Bildnis ist bezaubernd schön' from Mozart's *Magic Flute*, in which the singer gazes at a portrait and sees what he wants to see.

'After *Fitzcarraldo*,' Herzog recalls, 'I did go to opera once or twice and several houses asked me to come and direct. But at first I said "No".'

Eventually, though, Herzog succumbed, and his début as an operatic director took place in Bologna in 1985, when he took charge of a new production of Busoni's *Doktor Faustus*. Since then, his operatic credits have included Verdi's *Giovanna d'Arco* in Bologna ('a *bordello* of a text!'), Rossini's *La Donna del Lago* at La Scala, Milan, and two operas by Wagner: *Lohengrin* in Bayreuth and *The Flying Dutchman* in Paris. 'I now think Wagner is the greatest of them all!' laughs this latter-day convert to the Master.

Are his own movies 'operatic'? He doesn't think the adjective applies (except to *Fitzcarraldo* where the most important character, he says, is the voice of Caruso—a permanent, unseen presence in the drama). Many of them do, however, portray fiercely determined, flawed individuals as they struggle with large, basic emotions. There are massively choreographed crowd scenes in some films, and frequent incidents of capture and rescue. Also, in his locations, Herzog, like many opera composers, has displayed a *penchant* for challenging and exotic settings on the rough edges of civilization—in his case, the deserts of Africa and the dark and threatening forestlands of Latin America. Watching his films, it is hard to avoid the conclusion that Herzog feels he could not create anything really worthwhile unless he and his team were first to encounter the challenge of genuine danger.

159

Domingo, too, if not attracted to danger, loves a challenge. At 53, after nearly 2500 operatic performances of over 100 roles, he might be forgiven for wanting to repeat earlier triumphs. Not a bit of it: 'At the moment I am learning more new operas,' he told me, 'than at any time since the beginning of my career.' In 1994–5 alone, after *Il Guarany*, he had plans to perform Massenet's *Hérodiade*, Mozart's *Idomeneo* and Verdi's *Simon Boccanegra* on stage for the first time, and to record Mahler's *Das Lied von der Erde*, and two further operas: Gounod's *Roméo et Juliette* and Puccini's early work *Edgar*. Having recently added Wagner's *Die Walküre* to his repertoire, he is scheduled to conduct *The Flying Dutchman* for the first time in 1995 and sing his first *Tristan und Isolde* in 1996. Domingo also likes to visit countries and opera houses hitherto unfamiliar to him. He has sung in Rio and São Paulo. But he has long said that one of his greatest ambitions (which was nearly fulfilled on one trip to Brazil and only thwarted by an ill-timed devaluation of the Brazilian currency) is to bring opera once again to Manaus.

How would Herzog, whose movies so often feature a driven child of nature confronted and constricted by the deadening hand of 'civilization', draw from the greatest actor-singer of modern times a 'noble savage' emerging from the forestlands of Brazil? The encounter between the superstar of the opera stage and the *cinéaste* of ultimate danger was keenly awaited.

During early rehearsals, Domingo was mostly absent as he commuted between Vienna (where he was conducting *I Puritani*), London (singing *Carmen*) and Paris (singing *Tosca*). His schedule for May 1994 — the month immediately preceding the *Guarany* opening — looked like this:

2 May: Vienna: *I Puritani*

4 May: Monte Carlo: Lifetime Music Achievement Award

5 May: Vienna: *I Puritani*

6, 7 May: Vienna: 'Plácido Domingo World Competition' sessions

160

8 May: Vienna: daytime: Competition semi-finals

           evening: *I Puritani*

9 May: London: rehearsal of *Carmen*

10 May: London: *Carmen*

11 May: Vienna: *I Puritani*

12 May: Bonn: rehearsal of *Il Guarany*

14 May: London: *Carmen*

15 May: Vienna: *I Puritani*

17 May: London: *Carmen*

18 May: Vienna: *I Puritani*

20 May: London: *Carmen*

21 May: Bonn: rehearsal of *Il Guarany*

22 May: Paris: film tribute to Charles Aznavour

24 May: Paris: rehearsal of *Tosca*

25 May: Bonn: rehearsal of *Il Guarany* (Paris *Tosca* cancelled because of strike)

27 May: Paris: *Tosca*

30 May: Paris: *Tosca*

31 May: Bonn: *Il Guarany* press conference and rehearsal.

At most of the early rehearsals of *Il Guarany*, and some of the later ones, the part of Pery was played by the indefatigable Antonio Lotti, a cheerful, barrel-chested tenor from Brazil who was also singing the lead in *Tosca* between times. Lotti once sang the role of Pery in a concert performance back home and is thus the only person in the entire *Guarany* team who had ever taken part in a performance of the opera before. He was due to take over the part of Pery once Domingo had sung his four scheduled performances.

Whenever Domingo did manage to put in the occasional day in Bonn to join his *Guarany* colleagues, his presence would invariably give a perceptible 'lift' to everybody's spirits, even though he had not yet mastered the long and demanding part of Pery — especially the text — and needed periodic prompting. But Domingo learns fast and at these early sessions he was all dark-eyed Latin confidence and charm, waving to Neschling and Herzog and positively beaming at the talented international cast of young singers around him, who included the Chilean soprano Verónica Villarroel, the Spanish baritone Carlos Alvarez, Antonio Lotti from Brazil, a couple of

Americans and two basses from China and Croatia respectively.

He would chat animatedly in Spanish with Villarroel and Alvarez, two outstandingly gifted young protégés, and tell everyone in Bonn how these are the stars of the future. Villarroel, dark-haired and animated, with a rich, characterful soprano voice, sang opposite Domingo in the recording of *El Gato Montés*, a Spanish *zarzuela* piece dear to both of them, and has sung with him many times since. Alvarez (who also contributed to this remarkable recording) is still only twenty-seven and endowed with the voice, stage presence and sheer good looks required to establish him as *the* Verdi baritone of his generation, the natural successor of Sherrill Milnes and Renato Bruson. He has already been approached by Riccardo Muti to sing the title role of *Rigoletto* at La Scala. 'I like to think of them as my "children",' Plácido laughs. 'When you have been around in this business as long as I have, it is wonderful to know that there is so much talent in the next generation coming up behind you.'

He talks, too, about the recently established 'Plácido Domingo World Competition (Operalia)', which has already established itself as one of the foremost testing grounds for the young singers who will be the greats of tomorrow. There is no question that Domingo takes his emerging role as operatic elder statesman seriously. One only has to recall the care and commitment with which we saw him coach his young cast for *La Bohème* in Los Angeles. Domingo's periodic concerts of songs and arias are almost always given these days in company with younger singers: Verónica Villarroel, perhaps, or the Romanian soprano Angela Gheorghiu, whose careers have greatly benefited from their association with him.

What does Domingo think of *Il Guarany* now that the first night is only days away? 'It's a fine piece,' he says, with unfeigned enthusiasm. 'It may not be one of the greatest of operatic masterpieces. But it's like reviving one of the neglected works of Donizetti or Bellini, say, or Gluck.'

Why isn't it done more often?

'Well, it's very difficult vocally for all the singers, and dramatically, too — with its rather complex plot, *Guarany* is not easy to do. And I suppose if you have a cast really capable of doing it justice, then you'd be more inclined to use them for a production of something more familiar like *Don Carlos* or *Aida* or perhaps *La*

Gioconda—except that, unlike these, *Guarany* has no part for a mezzo soprano. But it does have great arias for all the principals, wonderful duets, powerful *concertato* parts for chorus . . . . Really, Gomes was a great composer!'

Was he a musician with a message? Is *Guarany* a 'green' opera, for example?

Domingo cautions against reading current concerns back into a nineteenth-century opera. '*Il Guarany* was written in the 1860s in Italy and set to an Italian libretto by a young Brazilian anxious to make his way in a world dominated by Verdi.' Then, reflecting on the 'noble savage' character he himself has to play, Domingo adds that Gomes was proud of the fact that his grandmother was a full-blooded Guarani Indian. Perhaps this suggests a clue to his message. 'I recall once meeting a man and asking him, "Are you from Paraguay?". He looked at me,' Domingo remembers, 'and said with great dignity, "I am an *Indian*!".' The memory of this brief encounter hovers around Domingo's consciousness throughout rehearsals as he tries to inject a sense of genuine pride into the character of Pery.

The inspiration for the opera was the romantic novel, *O Guarani*, by José de Alencar (published in 1857). To this day, Alencar's central characters, Pery and 'Ceci', are familiar to every Brazilian schoolchild. Like Romeo and Juliet, they have become archetypes—the white girl and her native lover—and have often been represented in popular books, songs and films and are regularly incarnated at carnival time.

When the novel was written, Brazil had recently become independent from Portugal and was governed by a cultured and enlightened ruler, Pedro II. Alencar and his contemporaries, responding to the climate of the times, developed a form of romantic, nationalistic art that reached its apogee in *O Guarani*. It was, therefore, bold of the young Carlos Gomes, a decade later, to turn to this great novel as the basis for his opera—a measure of his confidence, perhaps, and also of his desire to bring the flower of Brazilian culture to the attention of his European contemporaries.

Gomes had already composed two other operas, both written to Portuguese libretti, but he was now living in Italy and, if he was to flourish there, he knew that he would have to set Italian texts. Thus,

Alencar's novel, somewhat stripped of its more reflective, poetical elements, was turned by Gomes' friend and colleague, Antonio Scalvini (with additional contributions from Carlo d'Ormeville), into a rip-roaring Italian libretto. Gone were Pery's vision, in the smouldering ruins of a house put to the torch, of the Virgin — the dream that became reality when he first encountered and saved the life of Cecilia. Pery's name for Cecilia in the novel — 'Ceci', meaning 'Sadness' in the Guarani language — is a subtlety lost in the opera. Also, Alencar's evil Italian missionary, seduced by lust for silver, was diplomatically replaced by a more acceptable foreigner, a Spaniard named 'Gonzales' (sung at the work's première in 1870 by the French baritone Victor Maurel, later to be Verdi's first Iago and Falstaff). The result is a plot packed with the swaggering action that was *de rigueur* on the operatic stages of the time, and a cascade of magnificent, catchy music in an idiom that all could enjoy at a single hearing.

At the première at La Scala, Gomes is said to have taken refuge high in the theatre's fly tower, contemplating suicide if the show was a failure. Instead, it was a huge success and the composer became an instant celebrity. Cartoonists portrayed him as a richly exotic creature with feathers in his hair, and the librettist Antonio Ghislanzoni (who was to collaborate with Gomes on his next two operas) wrote of him:

> This wild man, elegant and capricious, who sometimes crouches, jackal-like, among the camellia and hydrangea bushes, has one of the most honest and generous natures I have ever encountered. Have no fear! Shake his hand with confidence and affection!

Even the cautious Verdi was moved to compliment the young man on *Il Guarany* when he heard it in 1872. Within a few years, *Guarany* was being produced at virtually every important opera house in the world (including Covent Garden in 1872 and the newly-opened Metropolitan Opera, New York, in 1884).

Gomes went on to compose a number of other important operas, but was never able to cap his initial triumph. In later life, he became caught up in a number of personal and financial tangles that seem to have drained his creative energies and he died in Brazil in 1896 aged sixty.

When did Neschling first hear the music of *Il Guarany*? 'I was born with *Guarany*,' he jokes, recalling how, as a child, he knew the first eight bars of the overture because they were used as the signature tune of Brazil's seven o'clock news programme. 'When I heard *Guarany*, I knew it was time to turn off the radio!'.

To this day, the *Guarany* overture is familiar throughout Brazil and a popular concert item. And if you are familiar with the overture, you already know many of the opera's best tunes including the rising $\frac{4}{4}$ figure that constitutes the essence of the famous Cecilia–Pery love duet in Act I (recorded by Caruso and Destinn in 1914). The curtain rises to the music of a hunting chorus (shades of *Der Freischütz*, *Don Carlos* and many others) and, before long, we are introduced to the principal characters. Pery appears and announces himself over a recurring Indian motif, and when Cecilia arrives she is given an entry aria with a catchy Polish rhythm (not unlike the *polacca* in *I Puritani*). During the course of the evening, the chorus have an 'Ave Maria' to sing at knee bend, an exotically harmonized 'ethnic' chorus, and a couple of frantic calls to arms — all in the best traditions of Verdi — while the evil Gonzales, in addition to swearing false oaths and trying to abduct beautiful but reluctant girls, has an absolute showstopper of an aria that includes swaggering Spanish rhythms reminiscent of a fandango.

As for Pery, he is on stage for much of a long evening, participating in two duets with Cecilia, one with Gonzales and another with Cecilia's father. Pery's one solo aria occurs at the beginning of Act II ('Vanto io pur'), where he reflects on the contrast between Cecilia's origins and his own, but there is scarcely an ensemble in which he does not participate. The *tessitura* is demanding, much of the writing lying on the natural 'break' in the tenor voice, while dramatically, the part requires the ardour of a lover and the dignity and pride of a native Indian who is true to his race and also to his convictions.

Pery is the only Guarani Indian we see on stage, but there is another Indian tribe — the Aimorè — who are represented from the outset as the 'baddies'. They are almost an extension of the forest — naked, primeval, threatening, savage, cannibalistic, consuming everything in their path, like the vast, dark vegetation.

Act III of *Il Guarany* takes place in the Aimorè camp. Cecilia has been captured and is held prisoner as the Aimorè pour out their scorn for the Portuguese. Suddenly, Pery appears, and is immediately held by Aimorè warriors. The confrontation between the barbarous Aimorè and the noble Guarani leader is a scene to which Domingo and Herzog devoted a great deal of attention at early rehearsals. These were held in the 'Probebühne', the stage-sized rehearsal studio just off the corridors that house Bonn Opera's administrative offices. Enter the Probebühne and you see a large bare, cubic space with black curtains over otherwise bare walls, with air-conditioning pipes visible against the ceiling and rudimentary 'scenery' scattered at strategic points around the floor space. A group of about fifty men and women, accoutred in different degrees of informality, stand or sit in clusters. Most wear jeans and loose shirts; many will be wearing a great deal less by the opening night.

Some of the men carry jagged-topped spears that they wield benignly enough. Others tote rifles with which they pretend to threaten their clearly unintimidated colleagues. Watching them, wandering among them, brown hair and moustache neatly trimmed, is Herzog—active, watchful, healthy and upright in his gait. He moves the women a little, so that they will be more clearly visible, and asks the riflemen to return their weapons, as they are going back to the beginning of the scene.

The Probebühne may be the size of the opera house stage, but it is certainly no bigger. The relay of people attending the proceedings—a couple of the soloists who are not needed for the moment, the chorus master, conductor and assistant conductor and members of the production team—all have to make themselves scarce on a neat row of chairs lined up near the doorway. At the far end, tucked with his instrument into a dingy corner, is one of those tireless rehearsal pianists without whom no opera house could function. These are the people in the bleachers, the bunkers, the sidelines, watching the midfield play, as it were. Yet they, too, have their prescribed and proscribed activities, territories and movements. The pianist plays, the conductor beats time, his assistant prompts the singers with verbal cues, and Herzog moves as and where he wishes. Everybody's role is assigned, known, unwritten, unbroken. There is the goodwill of a shared enterprise that everybody wishes to get right.

'You don't need to struggle here,' Herzog tells Domingo as they work with the Aimorè spear-carriers to establish exactly how Pery should be arrested. 'Remember, you've come here, proudly, of your own free will, to rescue Cecilia.' Always, the pride of the Guarani is foremost. 'You will come down a long ramp from the back of the stage, Plácido, and confront the Aimorè. Then you will be held by your arms — like this . . . Is that O K for singing?' Domingo nods approvingly. Then, Pery has to be allowed to move down stage for his confrontation with the Aimorè 'Cacico' or chieftain.

The Cacico, having earlier proposed to make Cecilia his queen, is furious at this intruder from another Indian tribe who wants to rescue her. He announces angrily that Pery will provide the Aimorè elders with a banquet that night ('Plácido's lost so much weight,' laughs del Monaco, 'that we should have cast Pavarotti in the role of Pery!').

The two captives — Cecilia and Pery — are briefly left alone and Pery, it seems, is required by the story to take poison, but the score and text do not indicate precisely where or why.

Domingo is perplexed: 'What I know at this point is that they are going to cook me for dinner. They're going to make me really well done!' Everybody laughs at the absurd prospect. 'But I don't think the public will understand if I just take out a bottle of poison and drink it.'

Neschling agrees, and adds that they will be even more confused in the next Act when they see Pery alive and well. There is a brief reference to his having taken an antidote once he and Cecilia were safely out of the clutches of the Aimorè, but this, too, is something that audiences could easily miss.

Why does Pery take poison? To ensure that all who eat him will also die? And where does he get the poison from? Should one of the Aimorè give it to him? At what point should he drink it? Should Cecilia see?

Domingo, Villarroel, Herzog and Neschling go into a huddle to discuss the score, the text, the storyline, the characters and the motivation: 'You know, while I am with Cecilia singing this duet,' Domingo feels, 'I am surely a little bit optimistic or happy, if only briefly. It would be very odd to take poison, just like that, in the middle of a love duet.'

167

The clock shows that it is time for a break. Spears and cloaks are placed back in their cupboards and the chorus of Aimorè cannibals go off to consume nothing more offensive than a slice of pizza and a coffee. Villarroel and Domingo chat in Spanish about a forthcoming concert together in Mexico ('Let's do this duet', they agree). Herzog discusses the props they will need for the rehearsal of the final Act, while Neschling goes off to prepare for tomorrow morning's orchestral rehearsal.

The Beethovenhalle Orchestra is a fine ensemble that gives a regular season of symphony concerts under its current Musical Director, the American conductor Dennis Russell Davies. They (and he) also appear regularly with the Bonn Opera and are familiar with the standard repertoire. But *Guarany* is new and unfamiliar territory, and Neschling gives the orchestra a tough time, knowing, as they all do, that these performances are to be recorded (by Sony) and will therefore reach a public far beyond those able to attend in Bonn.

Il Guarany is a long opera and Neschling was keen to open up some of the cuts that had been observed in earlier performances of the work. However, when he saw the ragged state of the orchestral parts from which he and the players had to work he was appalled. Thus, the first three or four rehearsals with the orchestra had to be devoted almost entirely to the frustrating business of correcting errors in the printed parts, and it was hardly surprising if some members of the band initially found it difficult to get to grips with the piece. 'It's richly orchestrated,' Neschling says, 'and full of rhythmic ingenuity and harmonic surprises — not easy for the orchestra. And we weren't able to get down to proper music making until we'd first done ten or a dozen hours of correcting.'

Is *Guarany* basically an Italian opera that just happens to have been written by a Brazilian composer, or are there authentically Brazilian qualities in the writing?

'It's an Italian piece,' he answers, 'with many of the qualities you associate with Ponchielli, say. But remember that Gomes was deeply affected by Meyerbeer and the French School, and was also profoundly influenced by Wagner. Indeed, his next opera, *Fosca*, was criticized as being "too Wagnerian". So you can say that Gomes is very much a product of the dominant European operatic traditions of the time. And yet there are Brazilian elements in *Guarany* as well.'

I presumed that these came in the form of the 'Indian' themes for Pery or the 'savage' music, complete with screaming piccolo effects and discordant semitone runs, associated with the Aimorè Indians.

Not really, says Neschling. These are largely pastiche, like the supposedly 'exotic' or 'ethnic' sounds you get in operas like *L'Africaine*, *The Pearl Fishers*, *Faust*, or *Samson et Dalila* (or Verdi's early piece about an Inca princess, *Alzira*). Gomes knew little or nothing, it seems, about the music of the Brazilian Amerindians, whereas Verdi, when writing the ballet music for *Aida*, made some attempt to learn about the musical traditions of Egypt, and Puccini, a few years later, tried to incorporate authentically 'Japanese' and 'Chinese' effects in *Madama Butterfly* and *Turandot*.

'No, it's not the "native" effects that are especially Brazilian,' Neschling continues, nor of course had Gomes absorbed any of the Negro rhythms that were to play an important part in Brazilian music of the twentieth century. What Gomes' music *does* reflect, he believes, is the Portuguese *cantilena* — with its long melodic phrasing and characteristic harmonic turns — that was typical of much Brazilian music at the time (and was to feed into the music of Villa-Lobos and other Brazilian composers later on). Neschling cites as an example the aria in which the Cacico proposes to make Cecilia his queen: 'Just like a traditional Brazilian *berceuse*', he feels.

Il Guarany is clearly something of a mission for Neschling, who relishes this opportunity to put his stamp on what will surely be an historic event. 'If this really comes off,' he says, 'it could be the start of a world-wide Gomes revival,' and he talks with informed affection of some of Gomes' later operas. '*Guarany* is a good score,' he insists, as he goes back into rehearsal, 'an interesting score, difficult to pull off — but,' he emphasizes, 'at least as good as all those operas by people like Giordano or Cilèa!'.

Neschling was thinking of works like Cilèa's *Adriana Lecouvreur* and Giordano's *Andrea Chénier* and *Fedora*, which have enjoyed a vogue in recent years, especially when outstanding singers have been available who are capable of breathing life into these hothouse products. But they are not standard repertoire. Most opera houses continue to rely on a small core of popular masterworks by Mozart, Verdi, Wagner, Puccini, Strauss and a handful of others. However, any house with serious artistic ambitions, in addition to producing *Trovatore* and *Tosca*, *Barbiere* and *Bohème*, *Figaro* and *Faust*, *Rigoletto*, *Rheingold* and *Rosenkavalier*, will also want to widen its repertoire, moving out of the mainstream, commissioning the occasional new opera and, above all, as here in Bonn, reviving interesting but under-exposed works from the past.

This can represent various levels of risk. Every seasoned opera-lover is familiar with the experience of trying out a new or unfamiliar work, entering the theatre open-minded and optimistic, and leaving disgruntled three hours later, beset by the nagging conviction that 'the old favourites are the best'. Nor does the promotion of little-known works normally bring more than temporary glory to managements who, even if applauded at first for their artistic temerity, can find themselves playing to empty houses and criticized for bad bookkeeping. Everybody is thus pressed back into playing safe, and opera is widely regarded as a 'museum art', a temple devoted to icons from a distant past, with the same handful of venerated works performed again and again, in the standard way.

How far is this image justified? Is opera as practised in the late twentieth century a fossilized art, a series of dated lab exhibits pickled in the stale formaldehyde of their own past? Do artists, managements and audiences treat opera as a kind of fundamentalist religion in which (pending the arrival of a new Messiah) they take regular and ritualistic sustenance from communion with the holy relics from an earlier and greater era? And how does the revival of a forgotten work like *Il Guarany* fit into such a picture?

The caricature does contain a degree of truth. There is no doubt, for example, that many operagoers *want* to see the same old works done in the same old way again and again, almost as though fearful that the old religion might die unless the faithful continue to tend the flame. And there can be something almost ritualistic about a powerful performance of *Norma*, *Aida*, *Parsifal* or *Turandot*, a formalized re-enactment of a great mythic story created by a revered figure from the past, in which our visual and aural imagination is stimulated by powerful emotions of a transcendent nature. The emotional catharsis involved is akin to that experienced by the devout in church.

Yet this is only part of the truth. Far from becoming the preserve of a minority anxious to retain the rituals of a dying past at all costs, opera in recent years has enjoyed an unprecedented burgeoning of popular interest. Opera companies and audiences are far more numerous than ever before. When I started going, forty-five years ago, there was one full-time company in Britain; today there are some half-a-dozen. In the United States, as in France, Germany and Italy, there is opera in most major cities and many minor ones, while opera is now big business in places like Australia and Japan.

Radio, television and record companies report a huge upswing in the popularity of classical music in general and opera in particular, a trend confirmed by the proliferation of glossy magazines devoted to the latest CDs, videocassettes and laser discs. The phenomenal success of the first 'Three Tenors' concert in 1990 and of subsequent sales of the sound and video recording, far outselling many more ostensibly 'popular' items in a highly competitive market, was a spectacular illustration. Music publicists have found themselves increasingly in demand to help fill the insatiable media appetite for news about the latest stars in the operatic firmament, and a major figure like Domingo is constantly besieged by requests for interviews.

In some ways, there is nothing new about this. Opera and the people who sang it have always reached out to a wide public. Rubini and Pasta, Patti, Caruso and Melba were supreme celebrities, fêted wherever they went, and massively rewarded for their talents, just as Joan Sutherland or Kiri Te Kanawa, Luciano Pavarotti or Plácido Domingo have been in our day. Furthermore, the stars of yesteryear were just as prepared as their successors to embrace the popular music of the time. Where Domingo sings the songs of Andrew Lloyd Webber, Caruso turned to the latest offerings by Tosti and made rousing recordings of 'Vieni sul Mar' ('Two Lovely Black Eyes') and George Cohan's 'Over There!'.

However, it is often said that the top singers of the past were drinking at the wellspring of opera, learning and performing new works straight from the pen of composers whom they knew and with whom they worked. Thus, Bellini composed the role of Norma with the voice and artistry of Giuditta Pasta very much in mind, Verdi those of Otello and Iago for Francesco Tamagno and Victor Maurel. When Puccini wrote *La Fanciulla del West* for the Metropolitan Opera, New York, he knew that the leading singers would be Destinn and Caruso and that the work would be conducted by Toscanini. Where, people ask, are the Rossinis and Wagners and Puccinis of today, pouring out one creative masterpiece after another for singers whose abilities they know and respect?

There are several answers to this question. For a start, much that Caruso and his contemporaries sang dated back fifty years or more. Caruso, in fact, appeared in only six opera premières, and sang far more operas by Donizetti than by Puccini. If you look at the repertoire of the great opera houses at the end of the last century and the beginning of this, they were more likely to be playing pieces already familiar to their audiences than the latest works by Mascagni, Franchetti, Giordano or Cilèa. The memoirs of Giulio Gatti-Casazza, who ran La Scala, Milan (1898–1908), and then the Metropolitan Opera, New York (1908–35), are full of complaints about the difficulties he had trying to persuade composers to write new works for him or his Board to agree to new works being mounted. After the great success of *Pelléas et Mélisande*, Debussy repeatedly promised Gatti that his next two operas would be written for the Met, but they never materialized. Boito took thirty years over his *Nerone*, but died with the work incomplete. The Paris Opera, anxious to encourage Charpentier after the success of *Louise*, eagerly produced his *Julien*, but it turned out to be a damp squib rather as the later works of Mascagni and Leoncavallo proved to be. Certainly, any new work by the mature Meyerbeer, Verdi or Puccini would be sure of an early airing, while Wagner, like Britten, would, in his later years, supervise performances of his own works under his own auspices. But we should not be misled by the genius of Verdi or Wagner into thinking that, at the time they were turning out their masterpieces, other composers of stature were also producing major works every year or two which were eagerly awaited by enthusiastic artists and audiences. The proportion of hits to misses has never been very high, and most performances most of the time, then as now, were of operas that had long since established themselves.

If the repertoire in the nineteenth century was not always growing quite as lustily as is sometimes supposed, the modern additions to it are not negligible. Only future generations will know, as we ourselves cannot, whether *Nixon in China*, *Gawain* or *The Ghosts at Versailles*, or the major works of Tippett, Henze, Berio, Reimann or Glass, will enter the repertoire as several of those of Britten have clearly done. Nor can we be sure how future guardians of 'serious culture' will regard popular works for the (mostly American) musical stage by people like Richard Rodgers or Stephen Sondheim — who are, essentially, successors to Johann Strauss II, Gilbert and Sullivan or Lehár rather than Verdi and Wagner.

Thirty years ago, it was almost unthinkable for a self-respecting opera house to mount a production of an American 'musical' or for an opera singer to perform these works except (like Ezio Pinza) in retirement. Today, artists of the stature of Jerry Hadley, Samuel Ramey, Frederica von Stade or Thomas Hampson explore the works of people like Rodgers and Hart or Cole Porter, while adventurous opera companies are prepared to consider including works like *Showboat*, *Kiss Me Kate*, *Sweeney Todd*, *My Fair Lady* or Bernstein's *Candide* or *West Side Story* — and the *zarzuelas* of Spain — in their repertoire.

Works like these, of course, precede the amplified rock culture of our own day, and there is no way that trained opera singers could easily enter the close-miked electronic territory inhabited by Metallica or Guns 'n' Roses. Nor, for that matter, are most opera singers comfortable in the more brutal chromaticism of the avant-garde. Domingo is quite frank about this, saying that he doubts whether operas like *Wozzeck* and *Lulu*, let alone those written in the more uncompromisingly atonal idiom associated with people like Stockhausen, will ever establish themselves with audiences the way that earlier, more obviously melismatic works have done. It takes real courage to write melodic music nowadays, he says, and he has tried to encourage Andrew Lloyd Webber, for example, to write a full-scale opera.

There are two further ways in which our own experience of

opera might be said to be expanding. The first concerns the growing importance in recent times of the operatic director or producer. Just as people talked with awe about Patti or Melba nights or of performances with Toscanini or Bruno Walter in the pit, people today talk of Patrice Chéreau's *Ring*, Giorgio Strehler's *Simon Boccanegra*, Jonathan Miller's *Rigoletto* or Trevor Nunn's *Porgy and Bess*. Gone are the days when a great singer would be invited to present 'his' *Pagliacci* or *Don Giovanni* at such-and-such a house, or when Adelina Patti could send an emissary to the stage rehearsal (if there was one) to inform the management what Madame wears and how she likes to perform this or that scene and to report back on the set and moves. Eva Turner once recalled to me how she used to be expected to travel round with her Turandot or Aida and Leonore costumes from one production to another, like a violinist or cellist with their instrument. Not so today: Chicago's Mimì, Iago or Kundry has to fit into an entirely different production and costume from that in Milan, Paris or Berlin. Gian-Carlo del Monaco told me that he had a chest full of his father's old costumes. Domingo does not own such a chest, as everywhere he sings he wears costumes that belong to that particular production and house.

This is controversial territory, and one is as likely to see an operatic masterpiece obscured as illuminated by the imposition of a directorial 'Concept'. Opera lore is replete with stories of perverse producers who imposed their own political or personal ideologies on works that had been created in an utterly different spirit, and any singer will tell you of grotesque and uncomfortable costumes they had to wear, physical contortions or dangers they had to undergo, all in the interests of a production with which they were utterly unsympathetic. However, there is nothing wrong in principle with 'concept' opera. There have been Flying Dutchmen who were entirely figments of Senta's fevered imagination, Scarpias from Fascist Italy, Macbeths from Communist Eastern Europe, ladylike Carmens and sluttish Mimìs — all, like Peter Sellars' provocative Mozart productions (*Così* in a roadside diner), interesting ideas that, if intelligently and sensitively pursued in the spirit of the music and not against it, can help bring a piece to life for a whole new generation of operagoers.

There is one other way in which our experience of opera seems to be wider than that of our predecessors, and that is in the redis-covery of works—like *Il Guarany*—often ignored by earlier gen-erations. Every era finds (and loses) older works. The mid-nineteenth century, for example, did not listen to Mozart's *Così fan Tutte*, nor the mid-twentieth to much Meyerbeer. However, the late twentieth century has proved remarkably eclectic in its tastes, not only pushing the boundaries of opera back to the time of Monteverdi and enjoying 'authentic' performances of hitherto rarely performed works by Purcell or Handel, but vastly expanding a bel canto rep-ertoire hitherto confined to a tiny handful of favourite works by Rossini, Bellini, and Donizetti. Verdi operas once considered rar-ities, like *Ernani, Luisa Miller, Simon Boccanegra* and even *Stiffelio*, have become accepted repertoire pieces, while a vogue for turn-of-the-century verismo has brought occasional revivals of pieces by composers like Cilèa and Giordano.

Many people deserve credit for this new eclecticism, not least a number of outstanding singers whose talents have helped push back the boundaries of operatic interest and taste. The bel canto revival, for example, owes much to the pioneering work of Maria Callas, Joan Sutherland, Marilyn Horne and Montserrat Caballé, who brought a fine legato line and dazzling coloratura to music that few had dared touch for generations, and which their successors consequently find less daunting. Among the men, tenors like Rockwell Blake and Chris Merritt and the outstandingly versatile bass Samuel Ramey have displayed a fleetness of touch that has encouraged imaginative managements to present operas by Rossini, Donizetti and others that had lain dormant for decades.

In the same way, Domingo, if not especially associated with the mining of unfamiliar seams of operatic ore, has always been stimulated by the idea of extending his repertoire and has performed many works that would probably not have been mounted but for his presence (such as the Met productions of Verdi's *Stiffelio* or Zan-donai's *Francesca da Rimini*). Any interest he expresses in taking on a new role, especially of a little-known work, obviously weighs heavily with operatic managements around the world. 'Il *What?* By Carlos *Who?*', many responded when Domingo first started mentioning *Guarany*. But some of them knew. And del Monaco was prepared to do something about it.

Opera may be a museum art, but, like all good museums, this one possesses far more fine exhibits than it can possibly show and, every now and then, a bold curator will re-examine the contents of the vast store cupboard, come across a forgotten gem, and decide to dust it down and display it to the public in a gleaming new exhibition case. When Domingo and his colleagues gathered on the banks of the Rhine in May 1994, they were confident that what they were shortly to unveil was something of real quality.

Rehearsals for *Il Guarany* are in their final week and have moved from the Probebühne to the main stage. The cast now find themselves dwarfed by a great craggy arch of dark, tropical vegetation, dappled by subtle lighting. Boughs and trunks of blackened trees, sun-starved but rain-drenched and overgrown with thick, dark mosses, form an arresting framework, while cankerous clumps of root, vast rubbery leaves or the snake-like hangings of jungle flora threaten from all directions to enmesh any mere humans who might trespass into this forbidden domain: a forest the white man has come to tame, but that looks well set to consume him first. As for the white man's intrusions into this all-enveloping ecology, they are indicated by the occasional introduction of iron filigree gates, a balustrade, a silken net or cluster of cushions. Props are simple but telling: a white-curtained parasol for Cecilia's entrance, a miniature puppet theatre for her to manipulate during her dreamy aria in Act II. The proscenium arch of the theatre is embellished for *Guarany* performances with a mottled black-grey stonework effect that parallels the minimal décor in the foyers of the Bonn opera house itself, and is reproduced on stage on the balustrade from which Cecilia sings her Act II aria.

Herzog — blue-eyed, slim, straight-backed, reserved, disciplined — watches everything, but by this point says little. From time to time he would slip on to and around the stage, adjusting the angle of a spear, helping one of the dancers to squat Indian-style on his heels or bringing Villarroel or Domingo further downstage. Then he would glide off the stage again, back to the director's desk in the middle of the stalls, thence to the back of the house, the sides, the wings. No sightline went untested.

'Opera is quite different from making films,' he emphasizes. 'In a film, everybody sees the same shot from the same camera at the same time But in the theatre, especially in opera, people have many things to concentrate on, and everybody is watching from a different seat.

'Directing film and directing opera have other differences,' he adds. 'Take the role of music, for example. In a movie, I decide what music to use and how it will fit the images I am filming. I may not always get it right. In the *Fitzcarraldo* screenplay, for example, I originally wrote that the central character is playing Wagner's *Die Walküre* on his wind-up gramophone. It seemed the right music for the effect I had in mind. But not when I was filming there in the forests of Brazil. It just didn't work. I found that Wagner and the jungle were *competing* with each other, fighting each other. But at least it was I who was choosing. In opera, on the other hand, a whole world has already been created by the music and the text, and I have to fit the images and the actions to these instead of the other way round.'

That evening, another three-hour rehearsal is scheduled. Again, Herzog says little, but would occasionally go up on to the stage, adjust the position of a giant leaf or bough, move someone into the light, press the chorus to remain motionless when not singing— all the time paring away at superfluity.

'Opera encapsulates human emotions in their most distilled, elemental form,' he feels, 'like the axioms of mathematics, reducible no further. That's why operatic emotions are so stylized—and so powerful. Opera,' he adds, warming to a familiar theme, 'involves danger, chaos, havoc, taking people to their limits and maybe beyond.' He is speaking of the characters on stage, but, one suspects, also of the hardworked singers impersonating them. 'So it's not surprising that the extravagant rubber millionaires built an opera house in Manaus even before they built a city. Operatic emotions and the tropical elements of Brazil go together,' says the creator of *Fitzcarraldo*, adding, after one particularly gruelling rehearsal, that a little danger here and there (the word he used was 'catastrophe') can bring out the best in an artist. He tells of a bibulous 'working dinner' during early rehearsals when one member of the team climbed up the furniture and fell heavily on another, injuring both, and adds with a wry smile that the incident was 'necessary to our work'.

The fourth Act of *Il Guarany* contains a remarkable scene between Pery and Cecilia's kindly father, Antonio (sung in Bonn by the sonorous-voiced Chinese bass, Hao Jiang Tian). Antonio's enemies are closing in on him, and Cecilia is once again under threat. Pery offers to rescue her, a proposition to which Antonio agrees, on condition that Pery converts to Christianity. Pery accepts, denounces his pagan beliefs and enters the church of Christ. The noble savage becomes a Christian and, therefore, earns the right to the white man's daughter.

This scene has to be handled with great sensitivity if it is to be convincing to modern audiences. Herzog has Domingo on his knees facing the audience, with Tian standing authoritatively behind him. Tian places his hands on Domingo's head, which looks good until he is reminded that Pery will be crowned by an enormous head-dress. Instead, Tian puts one hand on Domingo's shoulder and, with his other, withdraws a cross from his pocket. It is on this cross that Pery swears his new-found faith.

Should Domingo kiss the cross or, perhaps, hold it aloft? If not at this stage, maybe in the final tableau when Pery, carrying Cecilia, stands victorious in the light on a ramp at the back of the stage as everyone else dies? Herzog likes the idea as it would certainly make a wonderful visual effect, but on reflection, he feels that it would look too triumphant and so not really be true to the spirit of this final Act. 'Remember that by this stage we have only losers, not winners. Pery may have embraced Christianity, but he's also a renegade who has denounced his own culture in order to have Cecilia.'

Then perhaps Pery should hesitate before accepting Christianity, Domingo suggests, to show something of his mixed emotions. Pery is proud of his Guarani background, a man of great dignity ('the lion of the forest') who could never accept the white man's religion cynically, just to get the girl. But he also has a genuine and pure love for Cecilia and, perhaps, believes her religion must be superior to his own. In the novel, after all, Pery sees Cecilia as a romantic incarnation of the Virgin, and the love between the two of them is, by operatic standards, extraordinarily chaste.

Domingo sings through the music of the conversion scene to try and glean from Gomes' score some clues as to how he and Tian should play the duet. 'I think, at least at the moment when Pery accepts Christianity, that he really does believe in it,' Domingo says, as he swears allegiance to his new religion with shattering conviction—'Lo giuro! Lo giuro!'. 'Perhaps, now that Pery has seen the Aimorè,' he adds reflectively, 'he realizes that the Portuguese conquerors—and therefore their religion—are not so bad!'.

Neschling reminds them that, in the novel, Antonio's wife (who does not appear in the opera) detests Pery, saying that, like an animal, he has no soul. She only accepts him once he is baptized.

Herzog says, 'It goes back to the fundamental theological debate that took place in the sixteenth century about whether a native Indian could have a soul. To the Spanish and Portuguese conquerors of Latin America, the natives were not people but things, incapable of entering heaven unless they had been baptized.' This, he says, is the importance of the conversion scene. It is the moment when, theologically, Pery graduates from animal to human being, and of course, for nineteenth-century opera audiences, the scene served to differentiate Pery all the more from the Aimorè, who are killers, rapists and cannibals, and to make him, in effect, an honorary white man.

Herzog glances at the clock. Everyone is keen to reach the end of the opera if possible. Neschling goes back to his score, while Tian and Domingo re-adopt their conversion positions. 'O K,' says Herzog, summing up what they have decided, 'Pery doesn't grab the cross, he doesn't kiss the cross. And you, Tian, you just put it away back in your coat when the scene is finished. All right?'

They work on, finally reaching the cataclysmic end of the opera, though not yet with Herzog's spectacular and dangerous effects. These require rehearsal sessions all of their own.

As the first night approaches, tension perceptibly increases. The people from Sony arrive and set up their microphones as Neschling continues to work hard with the orchestra to iron out some of the remaining difficulties with Gomes' score. Villarroel develops a sore throat and spends two days quietly in her hotel room. Domingo, by now pouring intense vocal and dramatic commitment into the role of Pery, is still in need of the occasional prompt. Tall, hunched, lower lip curled and brow dark, he is by now all concentration. He tries on the costume Franz Blumauer has designed for him — long black Amerindian hair topped by a great luminescent orange head-dress, rows of beads around chest and waist, a natural-fabric war dress and Indian sandals all over a tattooed bodystocking. Do the dark feathers down his back make him too round-shouldered (like a giant bird)? Does the Indian war paint make his face too gaunt? He has lost a lot of weight in recent weeks, but might not the war dress look baggy?

The opening night of *Il Guarany* was to prove one of the most memorable at the Bonn Opera for years. A wealthy audience had paid up to four times the normal amount for tickets and, for once, every seat in the house was sold. Smartly dressed patrons assembled in the 'Pausenbuffet' and 'Rauchfoyer', downed their first glass of 'Sekt' and glanced at their programmes before filtering into the auditorium.

Backstage, Domingo adjusted his headdress and decided to dispense with one or two rows of beads, while del Monaco, resplendent in evening wear, came round to inject everyone with a shot of his own irrepressible optimism.

From the two minutes of tropical birdsong with which Herzog flooded the darkened auditorium before the beginning of the overture to the palpably dangerous crash of the portcullis in the dying seconds, the evening contained one *frisson* after another. The greatest, perhaps, was the slow wave of startled recognition that swept through the audience as they became aware of the identity of the dark, feathered figure who stole silently on to the stage early in Act I. Domingo went on to perform the part of Pery with total conviction, as though it had been in his repertoire for years, while Villarroel (all the better for being rested) and Alvarez triumphed with their showpiece arias. The final tableau was breathtaking as Antonio, Gonzales and the other adventurers were 'killed' by Herzog's spectacular explosions — while, gradually illuminated by the resulting flames, Pery, powerful and statuesque, became visible in the distance, holding the body of his beloved Cecilia, who had fainted (temporarily we must presume) as a result of all she had witnessed.

The performance received a rapturous ovation, and the cast had to return, separately and collectively, for a seemingly endless procession of curtain calls. One or two of the more earnest-minded in the audience were heard to mutter that they found *Guarany* 'improbable', while the politically correct of Bonn were confused by the portrayal of both 'good' and 'bad' Indians, and 'good' and 'bad' Portuguese conquerors (at least Herzog did not cut down the rainforests). Most, however, applauded a powerful evening of music theatre, imaginatively staged and superbly sung. 'This is a night of history,' Neschling enthused on stage afterwards as the curtain calls continued, 'the beginning of the Gomes revival!'

Del Monaco was thrilled, too: 'Nobody wanted to join us when we first proposed *Il Guarany*; now they're all going to want it!', and he reeled off a list of opera houses around the world who had already put in a bid to schedule his production.

Domingo, still wearing his headdress, padded over to Herzog and the two men embraced. Virtually in unison, they were heard to say: '*This* we have to take to Manaus!'.

It is easy to take Domingo for granted — always there, always performing, always outstandingly good, always charming and supportive. After the first night of *Guarany* there was a party over the road from the opera house at the popular Turkish 'Opera Cafe' for all concerned with the production. Domingo was due to fly off to Paris early the next day, but he was in exuberant mood at the party, helping himself from the excellent buffet-style spread, acknowledging the friendship and goodwill all around him. It was well into the early hours of the morning before he and Marta, surrounded by people craving one last brief moment of personal communion with the star — a touch, a smile, a kiss, a wave — finally showed signs of leaving. 'See you Wednesday', murmured one guest to Domingo; 'See you in Vienna', called another — or in Paris, London, Verona, Chicago, or Tokyo, next week, next month, next year. For decades, people have been taking Domingo for granted, routinely expecting more and more of the man, while at the same time waiting for him to burn out. 'They say' (I am sometimes told, almost conspiratorially) that on such-and-such an occasion Domingo sounded tired or did not characterize a particular role strongly enough. He shouldn't take on so much, his critics pronounce, shaking their heads gravely, just as they have for thirty years. Yet still they ask for more.

It would have been easy for Domingo to have decided, as virtually all other top singers do, to stick to a comfortable repertoire, perform it around the international circuit for as many years as the world's intendants and audiences wish, and take it easy between strenuous periods of performance. This is not a dishonourable course for an artist to follow, and some have become rich and famous in the process.

Domingo, though, has chosen to manage his career differently. Constantly on the lookout for new artistic peaks to climb, he is now deeply committed to a number of paths (German repertoire, conducting, the artistic direction of Washington Opera) that would have been unthinkable when he set out on his career. Evidently, he has retained, into his fifties, the voracious artistic hunger, and the phenomenal ability to satisfy that hunger, that originally propelled him to international stardom so many years ago.

Ultimately, however, it is not the variety of his achievements but their quality by which he will be judged. Domingo's voice is astonishingly unblemished by the passage of time, containing no hint of the wobble that often begins to afflict singers after years on the international circuit. The vocal versatility seems unimpaired, too. Listen to the recording of a concert he gave in November 1993 with the winners of the first Plácido Domingo Competition and you hear everything from the light elegance required for Gounod's *Faust* and the boyish agility of Nemorino in Donizetti's *L'Elisir d'Amore* to the dark, brooding quality needed for *Otello*.

As Domingo enters his mid-fifties, he remains capable of integrating music, drama and sheer vocal brilliance to a degree unmatched by anybody else of his generation. We have seen something of Domingo's astonishing artistry in the productions chronicled in this book (and the films it accompanies) as we have watched him struggling to master a new Wagner role, display his most famous portrayal with renewed clarity and breathe new life into a virtually unknown piece by a forgotten composer. And we have seen him on the podium, bringing the same intense musical intelligence to his conducting as he invariably displays as a singer; it is characteristic of Domingo to want to add to his conducting repertoire works that he has never sung, like *I Puritani* and *The Flying Dutchman*.

Domingo is a phenomenon of operatic history, virtually unique in both the range and the quality of his achievements. You might cite a major singer somewhere in the past who had a larger or wider repertoire or one whose acting you found more to your personal taste; you might choose to hear this or that voice rather than Domingo's in a particular role or repertoire, and there will doubtless also be other conductors whose work you prefer. Nobody, though, has ever before dominated so large a part of the operatic map as Domingo, bestriding it like a colossus.

Much of what Domingo undertakes at this stage in his career is filmed, recorded, or otherwise captured in one way or another for posterity. What we have tried to reveal here is something of the personal and artistic impetus and effort that lie behind his operatic triumphs, and something of the wider issues raised by his extraordinary career. For, just as today's opera lovers asked their parents and grandparents about Gigli and Melchior, and they pressed theirs about the Golden Age of Caruso and Jean de Reszke, future generations will thirst for tales from the Age of Plácido Domingo.

Index

Index